NOBODY UNDERSTANDS MY PAIN

NOBODY UNDERSTANDS MY PAIN

Dealing with the Effects of Physical, Emotional, and Sexual Abuse

LINDA HARRISS RN, LPC

Published in the United States
by Baxter Press, Friendswood, Texas.

Formatted by Rick Corrigan, Webster, Texas.

Cover design by Marcus Stallworth,
Stallworth Illustrations, Dallas, Texas.

ISBN: 1-888237-49-X

TABLE OF CONTENTS

ACKNOWLEDGMENTS

"I know the plans I have for you," declares the Lord,
". . . plans to give you hope and a future."
Jeremiah 29:11

*H*eavenly Father, I'll never be able to adequately express my gratitude to You for using the darkest days of my life to equip me to love and understand others who are experiencing deep pain. I will be eternally grateful for all that You have taught me on my incredible journey of faith. Thank You for Your undeserved, yet freely given, love, mercy, and grace.

Earl, my remarkable husband, thank you for believing in me more than I believe in myself and for being the wind beneath my wings. I will never understand the depth of your love and commitment to me. I am so blessed to be your wife.

My heartfelt thanks to Christie, Greg, Sally Sue, Raney Grace, and Caroline Rose for bringing indescribable love and joy to my life. Thank you for always encouraging and supporting me. I thank God for you every day. To Rose Mary Raney (my mom) for showing me by example how to love unconditionally and how to have a personal relationship with Christ. You have given me my greatest gifts. To Hughie Raney Sr. (Dad), thank you for teaching me to never stop until the job is done. To Delores, Hughie, and Paul for praying for me and for always being there for your "little sister." To Amber Raney (my niece), I could not have accomplished this project without you. Thank you for keeping my office and my life in order. To Grandmother Harriss (my mother-in-law) for teaching me how to have a servant's heart.

Thanks to Kathy Ide for her help in bringing this book together.

And to every client I've had the privilege of working with. You are my heroes and have been my greatest teachers. Thank you for allowing me to share your stories so that others will be encouraged and healed. I am so proud of you. Never stop believing.

INTRODUCTION

When Lauren[1] showed up for her first counseling session with me, she stated she had been depressed, lethargic, fearful, and filled with anger for years. She was troubled by recurring nightmares in which she was pursued by someone who wanted to hurt her. She had struggled with bouts of anorexia and bulimia from an early age. She felt guilty and shameful but didn't understand why.

"I've never been able to trust anyone," she explained as she sat on the overstuffed couch in my office. "I feel like I've been taken advantage of by everyone."

This young woman had been divorced twice and was on the verge of a third marital breakup. "Before my husband and I were married, I chose to become sexually involved with him. But since our marriage, I've had a real aversion to sex. And I have no idea what caused the change."

I recognized Lauren's fear, anxiety, low self-esteem, sleep disturbances, nightmares, depression, lethargy, anger, eating disorders, and inability to trust as common symptoms of abuse. As I continued with the initial session, Lauren told me about her addiction problems, withdrawal from family and friends, and her inordinate desire to please others. These details strengthened my suspicion that she was a victim of some form of abuse.

---

[1] Case studies presented throughout this book are composite accounts of actual patients' experiences. Names and details have been changed to protect privacy.

I asked Lauren if she had suffered any traumatic experiences from which she felt her life began a downward spiral.

"What do you mean?" she asked, looking intently at the dark green carpet.

"Lauren, have you ever been abused?"

"Of course not," she immediately protested.

I continued probing into her past, defining *traumatic experience* as "any situation or event that made you feel violated, dirty, nasty, and/or bad, anything that caused you to feel powerless, as if you had no control over your life."

Lauren shook her head. "No, I've never experienced anything like that."

I waited in silence for her to think back.

She seemed to focus for a while on a picture hanging on my office wall. It depicted a young girl sitting in a large, pastel-blue chair with a helpless look on her face. Finally, Lauren confessed, "When I was a little girl, my stepdad molested me. But I was very young. That has nothing to do with my life now. It's in the past."

I asked Lauren how she felt about the incident.

"It doesn't really bother me. I forgot all about it until just now."

"Did you ever tell anyone what happened to you?" I asked.

"I tried to tell my mom several times," Lauren said, "but she didn't believe me. My stepdad convinced her I was just a bad kid and that I was telling lies to try to force her to divorce him and remarry my father."

"Can you tell me how you felt when this took place?" I probed.

Her eyes misted. "Dirty. Powerless. Angry. And afraid. Somehow, I felt like I had done something wrong." Tears began to flow. "I haven't trusted anyone since then."

I offered her a tissue.

As she dried her eyes, Lauren said, "I feel like my whole life has been out of control. I've done things I never really wanted to do. It's like I'm always looking for something, but I don't know what it is. I just feel empty."

I watched the emotional battle reflected in Lauren's face under the soft light of the table lamp. "Lauren," I said, "there's always a reason behind unhealthy thinking and behavior."

"So maybe I'm not crazy after all?" she asked, the tears beginning to subside.

"Of course not," I assured her. "What you're feeling is quite normal for someone who has been abused. It's obvious that reflecting back on your life as a child is painful for you. Perhaps it's time to take a good look at the source of your pain so you can start to understand it."

This is how most of my counseling sessions begin. Patients are unable to associate their current problems with the source of their pain: the emotionally distressing experiences of their past.

Since going into private practice as a Licensed Professional Counselor, I have worked with numerous people who have suffered from deep emotional pain due to one or more traumatic incidents in their past. These experiences left them emotionally damaged, unable to function in a healthy state of mind, and many times behaving in violent, self-destructive ways.

I have also seen such people healed from the damage caused by abuse. Healing begins when victims are able to look back and determine what events triggered their painful symptoms.

Although the scars and memories of abuse never completely leave the individual, most can receive healing and enjoy fulfilling lives when they put their faith in God and allow Him to guide them through the process of healing.

Many of my counseling clients have begged me to use their stories in this book. The names and details have, of course, been changed to protect their privacy. But these are true stories of real people whose lives were transformed by seeking the help they needed to conquer and move beyond the haunting memories of their past.

My desire is that this book will help individuals who have experienced abuse, whether physical, sexual, mental, emotional, or spiritual. I pray that, through these pages, they will find hope and healing through Jesus Christ, by the power of understanding, perseverance, and forgiveness.

This book can also be helpful for those who work with abuse victims: lawyers, police officers, case workers, investigators, family, friends, and pastors who live and work with people who suffer from physical or emotional damage, and who feel that *nobody understands their pain.*

CHAPTER 1

CAUSES OF EMOTIONAL DAMAGE

*C*ountless individuals go through life carrying unbearable pain. Yet they are unable to explain their suffering to those around them. They cannot understand the reasons for their bizarre behavior and emotions. All they know is that something is wrong. Their world is upside down. Nothing is working the way it's supposed to. The everyday experiences of life—marriage, children, friendships, jobs—create intense stress, anger, frustration, and fear.

Perhaps you've experienced this yourself. *Nobody understands your pain.* You don't even understand it yourself.

A common thread runs deep through the hearts of people who suffer with depression, low self-esteem, unhealthy relationships, and addictions. Although these feelings may seem to appear out of nowhere, they are almost always rooted in a significant traumatic event, or series of events, that caused a breakdown in the person's ability to handle the normal experiences of life.

Usually, these events can be identified as some form of abuse—physical, mental, emotional, sexual, or a combination of these. The abusive event may be as simple as someone constantly demeaning you, calling you names, making you feel stupid or worthless. Perhaps someone you cared about hurt you physically, whether the pain was inflicted intentionally or not. You may feel sexually used by your spouse, significant other, friend, or family member.

I have even seen cases of "spiritual abuse" when Christians have torn apart a fellow believer's faith and destroyed his relationship with God over a sin, or perceived sin, that could have been overcome if the situation had been handled with understanding, kindness, love, and forgiveness.

Many times unhealthy behavior is an attempt to cope with abuse or some other devastating experience. Many people carry their pain silently for fear of being misunderstood, judged, or ostracized if the details of their past were made known.

Society tends to downplay the significance of abuse, causing victims to do the same. You know you're depressed. You feel worthless and different from everyone else, but you can't figure out why. When the subject of abuse is brought up, you deny having been abused, or claim that it didn't really affect you. You may compensate by trying to gain everyone's love and acceptance, or withdraw and live life isolated and alone.

Every day in my counseling practice, I encounter men and women who have suffered some form of abuse as a child, young person, or adult. When I initially meet with clients, I always ask questions about their past, attempting to determine if they had any traumatic experiences in childhood or young adulthood. More often than not, these people have been the victims of some form of abuse. And yet they make no connection between their past hurts and their present lives of turmoil, dysfunction, and pain.

TYPES OF ABUSE

Exploitation comes in many forms. Some types of abuse are blatant and apparent while others are confusing and less obvious. The word *abuse* describes any behavior that violates

16

or desecrates a person mentally, emotionally, physically, and/or sexually. The end result is intense pain, feelings of worthlessness, and loss of power in one's life.

Physical Abuse

Physical violence is the most easily recognized form of abuse. It includes hitting, kicking, slapping, pinching, shaking, biting, choking, or burning someone. It may involve use of a weapon such as a gun, knife, stick, lamp, or belt. Throwing objects, whether they hit another person or not. Shoving someone to the ground. Grabbing them by the hair or throat. Locking a person in a room or out of the house.

Physical abuse may result in bruises, cuts, scrapes, broken or cracked bones, ligament or tendon damage, black eyes, dislocations or sprains, concussions, broken teeth, nerve damage, double vision or blurred vision, difficulty breathing, miscarriage, gynecological difficulties, or damage to an unborn child.

Even if an act of violence causes you little or no physical pain, it can still be abusive behavior if it is done in anger, to control you, or to release the abuser's frustrations.

A husband's refusal to allow his wife or children to see a doctor when they are sick or injured is abusive behavior. Everyone has a right to competent medical care. If someone is forced to give up this basic right, and complications develop, the result is abuse.[2]

Benny, age seven, arrived for his first session with his mother, who reported that the young child's teacher had contacted her because his behavior was causing major problems in the classroom. Benny often hit people and shouted obscenities at his teachers and classmates if they refused to grant his wishes or if they confronted him in any way.

---

[2]   Catherine L. Scott, *Lovestruck: Realistic Help for Battered Wives and Bruised Homes* (Denver, Colo., Accent Books, 1988).

The boy's behavior at home was no better. He was often demanding and violent. His mother had begged her husband, Jerry, to allow her to take their son to the doctor, hoping the pediatrician would prescribe medication to curtail his outbursts. But Jerry refused to comply with her request. Every time she pleaded with Jerry about seeking medical help for their son, Jerry bristled in anger and reminded her that *he* was in control of his home. No doctor or anyone else was going to tell *him* how to raise his kids. He—*and he alone*—would decide when his family needed a doctor's help. He also feared that the doctor would notice the marks left on the children from his harsh spankings.

During my second session with Benny, I took out a large drawing pad and markers and asked him to draw a picture of his anger. He quickly and laboriously began creating a web of red and black marks with squiggly lines that connected and encircled each other. I praised him for his work and then said, "Benny, you have done a great job, but I still don't understand your anger. Can you tell me what it is like?"

With his big, blue, tear-filled eyes, he looked at me and said, "It's the big board inside of me that my daddy always spanked me with. I can't get it out. Can you help me get it out?" As I fought to hold back my tears, I assured Benny I would do everything in my power to help him.

When I asked Benny's mother to describe the father's behavior when he was angry, she began to cry. "Everything Benny does when he gets mad is what he has learned from his father. They have seen him beat me and they have experienced his violence, too."

According to the American Psychological Association, nearly one in three women will be physically assaulted by her partner during her adult years.[3] The National Coalition

---

[3] While abuse happens to both males and females, the majority of victims are female, and most perpetrators are men. Therefore, I regularly use feminine pronouns when referring to a victim of abuse and masculine pronouns for the initiators of abuse. However, these principles apply equally when the gender roles are reversed.

Against Domestic Violence estimates that one-third of all men who beat their wives also strike their children.

Between 1986 and 1993 the number of abused and neglected children more than doubled, from 1.4 million to over 2.8 million. During the same period, the number of children who were seriously injured by abuse rose 400 percent, from about 143,000 to nearly 570,000.[4] In 1991, 18,000 children were permanently disabled due to child abuse.[5] More than three children die each day as a result of maltreatment.[6]

A father or mother may justify abusive behavior toward a child under the umbrella of "discipline." While the law protects a parent's right to punish a disobedient child, including corporal punishment (spanking), that right does not extend to actions that result in injury such as welts, bruises, or abrasions.

Most often, a victim will deny abuse. She may admit that someone caused her injuries, but inwardly she believes she deserved the punishment. She may cover the bruises and try to avoid social contact until her wounds heal.

Abuse victims tend to give excuses to curious friends and relatives. When asked how she got that nasty cut on her head, a woman may say, "I tripped" or "I ran into a wall." If someone questions why her arm is black and blue, she may brush it off by saying, "I just bruise easily."

---

4   "Survey Shows Dramatic Increase in Child Abuse and Neglect, 1986-1993," *HHS News* (U.S. Department of Health and Human Services), September 18, 1996. (Web site: http://www.acf.dhhs.gov/news/press/1996/nis.htm.)

5   N. J. Baladerian, "Disability and the Family: Abuse Causes Disabilities," SPECTRUM Institute, Culver City, CA, 1991.

6   Barbara Tatem Kelley, Terence P. Thornberry, and Carolyn A. Smith, "In the Wake of Childhood Maltreatment," U.S. Department of Justice, Office of Justice Programs, Office of Juvenile Justice and Delinquency Prevention, Juvenile Prevention Bulletin, August 1997.

Three Phases of Physical Abuse

Physical abuse tends to follow a distinct pattern.[7] Incidents of violent behavior in a family take place in three identifiable phases.

In the *Tension-Building Phase,* an abuser will be irritable and critical of everyone around him. His wife and children try to avoid upsetting him by staying out of his way and/or complying with all of his demands.

The *Acute Battering Incident* could last for a few minutes or an entire day. The incident may be triggered by a casual comment or some minor disagreement. Whatever the inciting cause, the abuser reacts with unbridled destruction, raging out of control. This is the stage in which serious injury can occur.

The third phase consists of *Contrite, Loving Behavior.* The abuser becomes kind and solicitous. He expresses repentance, even though he may blame his wife or child for "forcing" him to "discipline" her. He may buy gifts and shower her with affection. During this phase, the wife or child may relax and feel that things are finally back to normal. But eventually, the abuser will give in to the pressure and frustrations of life. Tension builds, and the cycle repeats itself.

A man who physically abuses his family will probably continue in this behavior. If abuse has occurred more than once, it will most likely happen again. Domestic violence almost always escalates. Pushing and slapping progress to punching and choking. Bruises and scrapes become black eyes, broken ribs, and concussions. Biting and kicking lead to the use of fire and weapons. If the cycle is not stopped, the abuser may end up killing his victim.

---

[7] Lenore E. Walker, *The Battered Woman* (New York, NY: Harper & Row Publishers, 1979), 55–70.

Many women, especially those who are actively involved in a church or synagogue, feel trapped in their abusive marriages. Friends and spiritual leaders may tell a woman in this situation that God hates divorce and the Bible preaches strongly against it. They encourage her to simply "pray and have faith" that her situation will improve.

So she prays, fervently. She begs God to protect her from her abusive spouse. And yet, the cycle continues. She begins to wonder why God is not answering her heartfelt pleas.

Perhaps He has answered. In her heart she knows she must leave in order to survive. But her fear of the abuser, her dependency on him, and her desire to please God and others keeps her in the wounding relationship. She does not know how to live life without violence.

Some churches are now beginning to recognize abuse as grounds for divorce, or at least a temporary separation. There are times when it is vital to take active steps to protect yourself from caustic situations and/or dangerous people.

If you are the victim of abuse, how can you determine when separation or divorce is an acceptable, recommended, or wise course of action? That is a decision you must make for the safety of yourself and your children. Do not allow others to make that choice for you.

You may choose to stay with your husband because you feel you must try to "fix" him or "make him better." You may earnestly believe that things will improve if you just give him a little more time. This is certainly your choice to make. But if the circumstances don't change and the injuries continue, you should allow yourself to remain open to other alternatives.

Even if you choose to stay with your abusive spouse, at least remove your children from the hostile environment. This will take some planning, but it should be accomplished as soon as possible. Each incident of violent behavior that a child experiences will have a horrendous effect on her for the rest of her life. If you do not have family members or friends who can care for your children, contact Child Protective Services for assistance.

Mental/Emotional Abuse

Not all abuse is physical. Mental or emotional battering can be equally devastating. Angry words, manipulative actions or comments, and degrading name-calling are all attempts to confuse and/or control another person. For example, a husband may call his wife demeaning sexual names such as "whore" or "frigid" to humiliate her and make her feel inadequate. His disparaging comments make her feel responsible for all the problems in their marriage and family.

Your core beliefs about who you are, your personal value, and your self-esteem are deeply rooted in your mind and emotions. When spoken words are used as weapons, your sense of worth is destroyed. You feel hopeless, powerless, and trapped. Because you feel so worthless, you are grateful just to have someone in your life who will love you. Unfortunately, this demented "love" will only destroy you and steal your life. The longer you stay involved in this destructive relationship, the more difficult your recovery and healing will be.

Silence from an abuser can be as frightening as a verbal attack. It sends a message that the person receiving the silent treatment lacks value or worth. Your perceived lack of significance creates unbearable pain, which is reflected in feelings of guilt, shame, and responsibility for the abuser's behavior. Thus begins a downward spiral of low self-esteem, leaving you vulnerable to repeated victimization and destruction.

You feel terrified because you don't know what the abuser is thinking or planning. You become hyper-vigilant in your attempts to be safe. You try to make sure he is never agitated in any way. You "walk on eggshells," attempting to avoid any "triggers" that may escalate his anger. These triggers may be certain words or expressions that bring up unresolved issues from the past, any form of criticism, or something he may interpret as a personal attack.

You attempt to meet all of his demands of you as a wife and homemaker. The house is spotless, meals are prepared exactly as he requests them, and you dress in a manner that pleases him. Even the children recognize the cues and become quiet whenever he enters the room.

You fulfill his every desire, no matter the cost. Meeting his sexual needs is often traumatic for you, causing flashbacks to earlier sexual assaults that were the basis for your vulnerability to becoming a victim in the first place. Feelings of love, intimacy, and tenderness are nonexistent. You feel raped, emotionally and physically, but you endure the pain, hoping to avoid further violence, wrath, and emotional abuse.

You bear your anguish alone because your husband limits your outside relationships. He controls your actions, squelches your communication with others, even dictates your hobbies. He restricts your outside involvement, using jealousy to justify his actions.

You may interpret his jealousy as a form of love. You minimize your pain in order to justify staying in the relationship. You fear being alone, unloved, and unlovable.

Being abused at least tells you someone is there. You serve a purpose. You empower another person by staying and living with his violence. Without you in his life, your husband would feel insecure and powerless.

As the level and frequency of the verbal assaults intensify, you become dependent on the abuser, and he reinforces your belief that you can't make it without him. You reach a state of powerlessness, lack of control, and paralyzing fear.

Catherine, a fifty-four-year-old female, arrived at my counseling clinic deeply depressed. "I'm a failure," she told me. "I can't seem to do anything to make my marriage work."

I asked her to tell me about her husband. Jack, age fifty-six, was "a good man," according to Catherine. "Everybody likes him. He's very friendly." He served on several boards in the community—child welfare, the Hope Project for battered women, and the family preservation committee in their local church. "I know Jack could be just as caring in our home as he is in his volunteer work," Catherine said, "but I always mess up and stress him out when I don't do things right. I never get everything done that he needs me to do. I always fail him."

Catherine stated that she often made poor decisions and ended up making her husband get angry and lose control. "If I could just do things right, then he wouldn't have to yell at me. He's just trying to help me learn how to do things properly, but I always make him mad. He tells me I'm stupid. And I must be, because I keep doing the same dumb things over and over."

"Like what?" I asked.

"Forgetting to pick up his suits at the dry cleaners, for one thing. Yesterday, he asked me to make two appointments: one for his yearly physical, and one with the car mechanic. I didn't really forget; I just didn't take the time to do it. You see, I was sick and spent most of the day in bed with a fever. I should have made those calls, though. After all, he works all day and I don't do anything except take care of our home and do some volunteer work at the children's school and help out at the homeless shelter."

CAUSES OF EMOTIONAL DAMAGE

"It sounds like you're juggling several responsibilities," I said.

"I promised Jack I would give up my volunteering so I'd have more time to meet his needs."

"How did he respond?"

"He said I would be doing everyone a favor if I gave up my volunteer positions because I probably make a mess of everything there too."

"What else have you offered to do for Jack?"

"I told him I would get organized by making a list of things to be done and following it carefully."

"What did he say about that?"

"He laughed. He said he doubted that would work because I would probably forget where I put the list."

I asked Catherine what her greatest fear was.

She didn't hesitate. "I'm afraid Jack will leave me before I can make the changes he needs me to make. I can't survive without him. I just need him to give me a little time to get my act together."

When Jack ridiculed Catherine, his mind games overpowered her, making her feel humiliated and guilty. She believed she deserved to be punished because of the poor decisions and mistakes she made. She assumed that her husband's punishment would bring about much-needed changes in her behavior. She desperately wanted to make these changes in order to prevent Jack from becoming angry and upset again.

Because the traumatic relationship put constant stress on her emotions, Catherine's self-esteem plummeted while Jack's dominance skyrocketed.

Toward the end of our counseling session, I explored certain aspects of Catherine's family of origin. As we talked, she realized that she had never felt loved or accepted by her father, so she subconsciously looked for a man similar to him.

In the back of her mind, she reasoned that if she could do things right in her marriage, she would finally receive the love and affirmation she never received from her dad.

Catherine did end up marrying a man just like her father—one who abused her emotionally and degraded her sense of self-worth.

Sexual Abuse

Sexual abuse is one of the most devastating and traumatic experiences a person can suffer. It is the ultimate violation. It feels as if someone has reached deep inside you and ripped away your very life, leaving you with a sense of worthlessness and powerlessness, an inability to trust, and a complete lack of control. This violation leaves its victims experiencing life in a vacuum, numb and emotionally detached from others.

In my opinion, of all the traumatic events a person can experience, sexual abuse is the most misunderstood. Even after the physical damage heals, the victim must endure the laborious task of conquering the emotional and psychological devastation that has taken place. Professional help is required for the sexually abused person to find emotional and spiritual healing.

According to the Center Against Sexual Abuse, 38 percent of girls and 16 percent of boys are sexually abused before age eighteen. In 1994, 345,400 sexual abuse incidents in the United States were reported to Child Protective Services. But since 90 to 95 percent of all sexual abuse cases go unreported, the actual numbers are considerably higher.[8]

What Constitutes Sexual Abuse?

One reason some victims have difficulty acknowledging sexual abuse is a lack of understanding of what constitutes

---

[8]   Center Against Sexual Abuse, www.syspac.com/~casa/stats.htm.

abuse. They think that just because they weren't raped at gunpoint, they're not really a victim of this horrendous crime.

In essence, sexual abuse involves forcing another person to participate in sex acts against his or her free will. Sexual abuse of children is defined as "when any person, adult or child, forces, coerces, or threatens a child to have any form of sexual contact or to engage in any type of sexual activity at his or her direction."[9]

If a child or adult says no to any form of sexual advance, and the act is committed anyway, that person is a victim of sexual abuse. Some victims were unable to say no verbally because they were too afraid to argue with their attackers, or were numb to what was happening at the time, or did not realize this offense would affect their lives forever. Regardless of whether or not the victim specifically asked her attacker to stop, any sexual activity performed against one's will is emotionally and mentally damaging.

Sexual abuse comes in a variety of forms.[10]

(PLEASE NOTE: The following information contains graphic content and could be overwhelming for victims of sexual abuse. It may be offensive to some readers who are not familiar with the revolting details of being sexually exploited. If you believe you could be offended and/or further traumatized by reading these detailed descriptions, you may wish to skip this section and move on to the next section, *Progressions of Abuse*. However, an honest and forthright look at what happened in your past will, at some point, be necessary for your healing. So I encourage you to

---

9   Katheryn B. Hagans and Joyce Case, *When Your Child Has Been Molested* (Lexington Books, 1988), 21-22.

10   Suzanne M. Sgroi, M.D., *Handbook of Clinical Intervention in Child Sexual Abuse* (Lexington Books, D.C. Heath and Company, Lexington, MA, 1981).

read this section to see if anything on this list triggers memories of abuse that you need to acknowledge and deal with.)

The following definitions can apply to children, adolescents, or adults.

1. Adult Nudity

When an adult walks around the house naked, especially in front of young family members, that exposure can have damaging psychological consequences. Even brief disrobing in front of a child can be hazardous, especially when the child and the adult are alone.

2. Observation

When an adult or adolescent surreptitiously or overtly views someone undressing, bathing, excreting, or urinating, this constitutes abuse. The perpetrator may insist on watching the other person masturbate, or force her to look on while he masturbates, or arrange for both of them to observe each other masturbating simultaneously.

Forcing a person to disrobe, or to dress in a more sensual way than she is comfortable with, is also abusive behavior. Making someone look at pornographic magazines or videos against her will is abuse. Asking a minor to view, read, or participate in the production of pornographic materials constitutes child abuse. Exposure to pornography, the sexual activities of adults, or explicit sexual talk is an invasion of a child's emotional/psychological boundaries. Children are incapable of processing and handling such information.

3. Intimate Contact

Any unwanted or uncomfortable touching can be emotionally damaging.

A wife may avoid being in close proximity to her husband if he is constantly groping her. She avoids closeness to escape being used as a sex object.

An abusive adult might kiss a child in a lingering and intimate way, the type of kissing that should be reserved for adults. Such kissing is often followed by the adult fondling personal areas of the child's body and/or insisting that the child fondle him.

An abuser may perform such fondling while he thinks the child is asleep. Traumatic consequences result when a child awakens to find herself being fondled by a parent or other adult.

4. Genital Contact

If a man forces a woman to take his penis into her mouth, or insists on placing his mouth or tongue on her vaginal area without her consent, he is guilty of sexual abuse. If he engages in these activities with a minor, he becomes a child molester.

The same is true if the gender roles are reversed. A woman who takes a boy's penis into her mouth, or insists that he place his mouth or tongue on her vulva or in her vagina, is guilty of molestation. If a woman forces genital contact with an adult male, she is sexually abusing him. These acts may also occur between same-sex individuals.

5. "Dry intercourse" is a slang term describing an interaction in which a man rubs his penis against a woman's or girl's genital or rectal area, inner thighs, or buttocks, but does not penetrate.

6. Simply asking a child to have anal or oral sex (even if the act does not take place) is abusive.

7. Penetration

The most obvious form of sexual abuse involves penetration of the vagina or rectum by a perpetrator's penis, finger, or tongue.

Abusers may even thrust inanimate objects, such as vibrators, crayons, or pencils, inside the victim's body.

Even when offenders insist they were gentle and did not physically hurt the other person, these instances are all serious acts of abuse.

Rape

Rape occurs any time a person, male or female, is forced, tricked, or coerced into becoming a participant in sexual activity where vaginal, oral, or anal penetration takes place.

The horror of a rape remains indelibly etched in the mind and memories of its victim. While this crime is often attributed to strangers, most rapes occur within marriage, friendships, and dating relationships.

Rape happens to people of all ages. Infants, babies, and children. Males and females. Young people, adults, and the elderly. The healthy and the disabled.

One rape recovery center in Utah has worked with victims ranging in age from a 3-1/2-week-old infant to a ninety-four-year-old woman. On November 2, 1999, *Yahoo! News* carried a story about a forty-eight-year-old man charged with raping a fifteen-month-old child. The perpetrator even videotaped the incident.[11]

Accurate estimates are hard to come by. According to a 2002 report from the U.S. Department of Justice, only 36 percent of rapes are reported to the police.[12] The AMA estimates that about 700,000 women are raped each year,

---

[11] "Rape and Sexual Assault" brochure, The White Ribbon Campaign Organization, www.whiteribbon.com.

[12] Callie Marie Rennison, Ph.D., "Rape and Sexual Assault: Reporting to Police and Medical Attention, 1992-2000," Bureau of Justice Findings, U.S. Department of Justice, NCJ 194530, August 2002.

making sexual assault the most rapidly growing violent crime in America.[13] A 1998 National Violence Against Women survey estimated that one in six women has been raped in her lifetime.[14]

Most victims don't report the crime because society sends a message that women are responsible for men's behavior. The prevailing attitude within the general public is that women invite rape by the way they dress and act; they are, therefore, responsible for the crime against them. With this mentality, those involved in the legal system sometimes indicate that a woman who is raped simply "got what she was asking for."

Victims of rape usually fear that their perpetrators will either receive probation with a simple "slap on the hand" or go unpunished entirely. They may wonder if the humiliation of having the details of their traumatic experiences disclosed will be worth it.

In a sense, the victim receives a "death sentence" when the perpetrator walks free. Feeling unprotected emotionally and physically, she lives in constant fear of retaliation for reporting the crime. Her life becomes an unending nightmare.

The survey mentioned above also estimated that 111,300 men were raped in 1997. This is only an estimate because men rarely report rape. Most male victims are unable to define a sexual experience as being abusive or having a negative impact on their lives.

Society supports the idea that a man's identity is related to his prowess in the bedroom and by the number of sexual

13   "Rape in America: A Report to the Nation," National Victim Center and Crime Victims Research and Treatment Center, 1992.

14   Patricia Tjaden and Nancy Thoennes, "Prevalence, Incidence, and Consequences of Violence Against Women: Findings from the National Violence Against Women Survey," National Institute of Justice Centers for Disease Control and Prevention, U.S. Department of Justice, November 1998.

encounters he has engaged in. To admit that he was sexually assaulted, by a woman or a man, would make him appear weak. He would not be living up to the image of what it means to be a man.

In addition, society does not allow men to show any kind of emotion. Men are expected to ignore problem situations or to handle them quietly. There is no place for grief or acknowledgement of pain. Men are expected to be the protectors of themselves, their families, and others.

Men often fear that the consequences of disclosure would be more detrimental than remaining silent. *Nobody understands their pain,* so they suffer silently and alone.

Ultimately, the male victim is overcome with unexplainable anger, rage, confusion, and fear. Lacking the ability or approval to express his feelings, he takes on new behaviors. His options are limited to becoming powerless and passive or fearless and aggressive. If he stays in a powerless state, he remains a victim. If he becomes aggressive and angry, he recreates scenarios of abuse in which he feels in control. He may use illegal drugs and/or alcohol to gain a false sense of power, to block his pain, or to excuse his abuse of loved ones. Unable to control his feelings, he sees himself as a failure because men are supposed to be in control of their emotions at all times.

Whether the victim is a man or woman, rape is the ultimate betrayal. It rips away at the very foundation of your dignity, honor, and self-respect. The aftermath of rape is a sense of powerlessness, lack of control, anger, rage, dissociation, fear, and an inability to trust. The rape victim experiences a loss so deep it can only be explained as total emptiness, void of everything but indescribable pain.

Emma, a petite, pretty high school senior with brown hair and green eyes arrived for her first session in tears. She had become the target of a date rape by a college student named

Samuel, a star athlete from a nearby city. Their relationship began in a chat room on the Internet. Over a period of two months, Samuel convinced her to meet him at a restaurant midway between their hometowns.

After an enjoyable meal together, he convinced her to get into his vehicle to go meet his friends, who were camping at a state park nearby. Emma felt uncomfortable with the situation but convinced herself that she was just being paranoid.

As they left the restaurant, Samuel began making sexual comments and advances. Emma begged him to take her back to her car, but he persisted. Before long, she found herself alone with Samuel at an isolated spot on a country road.

After he raped her, Samuel took out a knife. He told Emma if she ever told anyone, he would kill her.

As Samuel was putting his clothes back on, Emma managed to get out of the car and ran, scantily dressed and barefoot, through the brush. She crouched behind a tree trunk and watched him drive back and forth, looking for her. A terrifying hour later, Samuel gave up and disappeared.

Finally, Emma saw a car coming. She ran to the road to flag down the driver for help. This Good Samaritan took her to a nearby hospital, where she was assessed and authorities were notified.

Months later, in a court of law, the rapist walked free. Influential people from the college town testified that Samuel was a good person and a great athlete. Emma was portrayed as a conniving and manipulative young girl who used sex to connect with a celebrity athlete. She left the courtroom feeling like she had been on trial and became victimized all over again.

Emma hated herself for reporting the crime. She felt labeled and marked by members of the community who continued to believe the lie that women are responsible for men's behavior.

PROGRESSION OF ABUSE

The typical scenario of abuse is a progression from less blatant forms of sexual activity (such as exposure and observation) to body contact (kissing and fondling) and finally to some form of penetration. Even the initial, relatively milder forms of abuse are damaging and painful.

When the abuse does not reach the more obvious stages, or when there is a gradual progression of abuse, the victim may struggle to identify the experience as abuse.

The greatest damage takes place on an emotional level. In many cases, what appear to be "milder" forms of abuse can be as destructive as the more "severe" types.

You may feel confused by the perpetrator's comments and behavior toward you. In your uncertainty, you tell yourself that you're reading too much into his sexual innuendos and advances. This is commonly referred to as "grooming." During this stage the abuser begins making subtle advances toward you, deceiving you into demeaning forms of sexual contact.

By manipulating you into participating in the sexual experience, the perpetrator accomplishes his goal of silencing you. He knows you feel responsible for what happened. Therefore, you will be reluctant to disclose your situation to anyone out of fear of what others will think, fear of what consequences may befall you, and fear that *nobody will understand your pain.*

RESULTS OF ABUSE

Because few people understand their pain, the victims of sexual abuse struggle through life feeling different from others and detached from the world. The majority of the population is unaware of the frequency of sexual abuse and its shocking effects. As a result, the injured person feels isolated, different, and alone. The fear of being judged and ostracized by family, friends, and society forces her to silently carry her pain and scars in a world that is oblivious to her needs.

Justine, a thirty-three-year-old woman, showed up at my counseling office in the middle of summer dressed in a long-sleeved jacket and turtleneck sweater. Since the outside temperature that day was 101 degrees with 90 percent humidity, I immediately became concerned. I introduced myself to her in the waiting area, and Justine greeted me without making eye contact. When I invited her to join me in the counseling room, I noticed that she grimaced when she stood. She walked with a slight limp, which she attempted to cover up.

"Justine," I said, "getting out of the chair and walking seem to be uncomfortable for you."

"Oh," she stuttered, "I fell down the stairs at my apartment. I landed on a toy that was left on the step."

As the session began, Justine asked who would know that she was coming to me for counseling. I explained the rights of client confidentiality, but my explanation did not seem to give her the assurance she needed.

"If my husband ever finds out I came here," she said in a shaky voice, "he'll be furious with me."

"If I reveal to anyone that you came for counseling," I explained calmly, "you have the right to contact the State Board for Professional Counselors and report that I breached confidentiality." I presented her with the State Board's address and telephone number. She gave a slight smile and thanked me.

As the session continued Justine spoke in a guarded manner, providing simple answers to the questions I asked. She gave me basic information about her family of origin, which she described as "poor nobodies." She reported that she dropped out of school at age seventeen to help support her family. Justine described her father as controlling and her mother as a submissive doormat. According to Justine her brothers were domineering, just like the father. She saw her family only on holidays.

Midway through her session, Justine dropped her glasses. When she bent down to pick them up, I noticed another grimace on her face. As she stretched to retrieve her glasses, the neckline of her sweater lowered slightly, revealing what appeared to be bruises around her throat.

I made notations of what I observed in Justine's body language. She sat with her arms tightly crossed over her abdomen, an obvious indication of a lack of trust. She tapped her foot as we talked and constantly tugged at the neck and sleeves of her sweater.

As I began asking Justine questions about her marriage, she told me what a wonderful man her husband was. "I'm just coming for counseling in order to work through my depression and be a better wife to Bill."

As I delved deeper into the relationship, she continued to stare at the floor and avoid eye contact with me. She looked as if she were on the verge of tears.

"Justine," I finally said, "I'm concerned that you may not be giving me an accurate description of your marriage. I'm troubled that you might be living in domestic violence."

For the first time during our visit, Justine looked up. She slowly took off her jacket and pushed up her sleeves. Her wrists and upper arms were covered with dark bruises in the shape of fingertips. She then pulled down the neck of her sweater, exposing more discolorations.

"Justine, where did those bruises come from?" I asked gently.

"When Bill gets angry with me," she said, her voice shaking, "he lifts me off the floor by my neck or arms and holds me up against the wall until I say I'm sorry. He won't let me down until I give in and take responsibility for his anger, and agree to have sex with him. Most of the time I give in before he bruises me." She paused, her eyes filling with tears of frustration. "This time I thought I'd rather die than give in."

"Do you want to have sex with him?" I asked.

"No!"

"Justine," I explained, "do you understand that anytime anyone forces you to have sexual intercourse against your will, it's rape? A violation. A crime committed against you. Marriage doesn't give another person permission to force you to engage in sexual activity against your will."

Justine blotted her eyes with a tissue. "I was always told that once I was married, my husband owned my body and I had to endure whatever he wanted from me. I thought sex, however he wanted it, was part of fulfilling my role as a wife." She started to sob again. "I hate the way I feel when he forces me to do things."

"What kind of things?" I prompted.

"Several times he has tried to make me have sex with other women or men. I gave in three or four times, but then I got so depressed about it, I thought about committing suicide." Justine finally looked me in the eye. "That's why I'm here today. I can't stand the pain any longer."

"Have you tried to talk to your pastor about this?" I asked, remembering that Justine had told me she attended church regularly.

"My pastor said that if I leave my husband, I will be going against God's will for my life."

I asked Justine if she told her pastor she was living in violence and abuse. She dropped her head. "I couldn't. He's a man of God. I felt despicable just being in his presence because of the filthiness of my life. I was afraid he would want me to leave the church so I wouldn't tarnish its reputation."

I explained to Justine that her fears of disclosing her abuse were common. But unless her pastor knew her circumstances, he could not give her proper counsel. I encouraged her to go back to her minister and share more openly the dilemmas of her life.

"I'm afraid my pastor won't believe me," Justine replied.

"I'll go with you if you like," I offered.

She stared at me for a long moment. "I don't know what kind of help he could offer anyway," she said. "He'll just tell me to stay with my husband because divorce is a sin."

I took a deep breath. "Justine, it's true that God never wants people to get divorced. But I do not believe that He intends for women to stay in relationships where they are being destroyed emotionally and physically." Her eyes glimmered with a spark of hope for the first time. "No one should make the decision for you regarding divorce, but I would recommend that you consider separation from Bill until you both receive counseling. Then, after much prayer, you can make a decision as to what to do about your marriage."

"I'd rather die than stay married to Bill," she admitted. "But I'm afraid that if I leave him, my church family will turn against me. They're all I have."

I encouraged Justine to be open with her Christian friends without feeling she had to give all the personal details to everyone.

"But what if nobody believes me or understands what I'm going through?" she moaned.

"You can't expect people to truly understand something they have never personally experienced," I explained. "But as you share your story, you may be surprised at how many others will disclose their own experiences of being abused.

Your admission could be the beginning of healing for other people who have never disclosed their abuse because they felt that *nobody would understand their pain.*"

The following week I accompanied Justine to visit her pastor. He was warm, empathetic, and caring. He praised her for having the courage to share openly what was taking place in her life. He also encouraged her to separate from Bill if he refused to seek counseling.

Justine ended up leaving her unrepentant husband. She is now making tremendous personal progress as she learns to understand and accept her value and worth.

THE CYCLE OF ABUSE

Once an incident of violence occurs in a relationship, tension and conflict escalate rapidly. As new patterns develop, an increase in frequency and seriousness is seen. Before long the cycle of violence becomes a regular pattern.[15]

The abuser releases tension by making emotional and sometimes physical threats. This allows him to gain a temporary sense of empowerment. But shortly thereafter, he experiences fear and a lack of control again. As this powerlessness resurfaces, the abuser feels vulnerable, and anger returns. When the level of anger reaches his personal threshold, he lashes out on those around him, attempting to place them in a powerless state again in order to regain control.

Unfortunately for those in relationships with abusers, there is no precise pattern for these sudden and unexpected explosions. It is easy to inadvertently push a perpetrator over his threshold by a spoken word or gesture that reminds him of the traumatic situation that left him feeling insecure and alone in life.

---

15   Peter H. Neidig and Dale H. Friedman, *Spouse Abuse* (Champaign, Ill., Research Press Company, 1984).

Warren, a twenty-four-year-old construction worker, sought counseling because he had begun to act abusively toward his wife, who was four months pregnant. He reported that when his wife announced she was expecting a baby, he was overwhelmed with anxiety. He resented the pregnancy and frequently vented his anger by launching verbal attacks on his wife. At times he feared he would physically abuse her. Memories of his childhood made him afraid he might abuse his own child.

Warren was one of six children, three girls and three boys. He was raised by an abusive father who was an attorney and a mother who was a withdrawn homemaker. Several times a week, Warren witnessed his father emotionally and physically abusing his mother. Following these beatings, the father would direct his abuse toward the children.

Warren's father rationalized his behavior, claiming he was being a responsible husband and parent. He said he had to discipline the children to keep them from breaking the law and going to prison.

He also said it was his place to teach the children about sex. During clothing changes and bath time, Warren's father would say, "Daddy loves you and has to make sure your body is nice and clean so you will grow up to be big and strong." Warren desperately wanted his father's love. But the inappropriate touching and words sent conflicting messages. Warren's concept of love became distorted by his father's cruel and selfish acts of molestation.

Thus began Warren's long and tragic journey of searching for the love he never received as a child. He attempted to find this missing piece of his life through various sexual encounters. Because the only way Warren received attention and validation from his father was through sexual means, Warren became vulnerable to perpetrators throughout his life.

When he was six years old, Warren was molested in a bathroom at a shopping mall by an older male while his mother stood outside the door, oblivious to what was happening. He never told anyone because the man said he would come looking for Warren and kill him or hurt his family members if he ever did.

Warren was also molested by a school bus driver, as he was the last student to be dropped off each day. This violation lasted for a year until Warren's sister started school and began riding the bus as well.

Warren also gave an account of incest among his siblings. Each child felt so confused about love and so totally powerless that they sought to gain love, power, and control through sexually abusing one another.

As the damaging cycle of incest continued, it left the confines of their home and extended like an epidemic into the lives of cousins and neighborhood children.

THE FUNDAMENTAL THEME

The absurd theme in all violent relationships is that the victim takes responsibility for initiating the abuse. This idea is planted and nurtured by the abuser.

Intimidation is frequently used to make the victim feel afraid through menacing looks and threatening gestures. The abuser constantly performs hostile acts such as destroying the victim's prized possessions, overpowering her, or aggressively invading her personal space by sitting or standing close to her against her will. He may display a weapon or his fist to create fear and anxiety. This fear leaves the woman feeling powerless and unable to abandon the violent relationship. She worries her perpetrator will track her down if she tries to escape. The punishment for abandoning him will be harsher than before. The victim learns to subsist in her world of violence. She knows only hopelessness, violence, abuse, and pain.

Several of the abused women I have worked with are "men haters." They feel a need to retaliate or punish males in general. Since they are too powerless to approach confident men, abused males who are weak and needy become their easy marks.

In some instances, men are violated in these same ways. An abused male feels powerless and insecure, which leaves him dependent on his female partner. His childhood may have been filled with rejection and criticism from a cold and distant father. Feeling unacceptable by other men because of his weakened condition, he seeks out women who exhibit power and the ability to protect him and give him significance in life.

THE POWERFUL EFFECTS OF ABUSE

Whether you are male or female, whether the abuse you have suffered is physical, mental, emotional or sexual, once the abuse has taken place, your mind and emotions become poisoned. For the rest of your life, every decision you make and every relationship you enter will be affected by this tragic event.

Because most people do not understand the behaviors of abused individuals, you may be judged, condemned, ostracized, and left to deal with your pain alone. This lack of support and understanding makes you vulnerable to further abuse, addictions, unhealthy relationships, and other self-destructive behaviors. Help can only come as you allow others insight into your life. Without their support and healing, your cycle of abuse will continue.

THE PROCESS OF HEALING

You do not need to suffer from the effects of the emotionally traumatic experiences in your past for the rest of your life. You can live a normal life, just like those who have never been abused.

The healing process must begin by acknowledging your pain and fears, making the decision to face your past, and identifying the root cause of your suffering. These are the initial steps toward the freedom you long for.

No matter what kind of horrendous experiences you have suffered, you can turn your tragedies into personal strengths and insights that can lead you into a deeper, richer, more meaningful life. If you are a victim of violence and abuse, at this very moment, I encourage you to make the decision to take your first step toward a life of freedom and healing.

SYMPTOMS OF ABUSE

*M*ost of the time, when an individual seeks counseling, she does not disclose her abuse right away. During my initial interviews, I watch carefully for indicators of the various types of abuse. Typically, an abused client will exhibit several of the following symptoms. Analyze yourself to determine if you struggle with any of these problems:

- **Low self-esteem** (feeling worthless and/or bad)

- **Addictions** (feeling you are out of control, being controlled by something or someone)

- **Abusive relationships** (abusing others or being abused, including self-mutilation)

- **Inability to trust** (emotionally or physically isolating or withdrawing from others)

- **Depression** (sadness, inactivity, feeling emotionally detached or numb, sometimes resulting in an inability to concentrate and/or a drop in school or work performance)

- **Controlling behaviors** (feeling powerless, choosing behaviors that result in a sense of empowerment such as controlling others, stealing, setting fires, or lying)

- **Anxiety and/or fear** (worry about potential future abuse; may come out in dreams, isolating yourself from others, or in health-related problems such as high blood pressure, panic attacks, insomnia, ulcers or gastrointestinal problems)

- **Boundary issues** (confusion as to where your personal space begins and ends, difficulty protecting your personal space and not intruding into the personal space of others)

- **Guilt and/or shame** (feeling responsible for something you didn't do or for what someone has done to you)

- **Sense of powerlessness** (may be shown through anger, fear, and/or perfectionism)

- **Intimacy problems** (unhealthy relationships including promiscuity, sexual difficulties, excessive masturbation)

The most prevalent symptoms of abuse are low self-esteem, addictions, and the existence of abuse in present relationships. In the next three chapters, I will deal with each of these symptoms in depth. First, I would like to address a few of the other symptoms.

INABILITY TO TRUST

Trust is foundational to all relationships in life. Unfortunately, people who have experienced abusive situations soon lose their ability to trust. When an incident involves an attack from someone you know and love, the sense of loss is even greater. You innately believe you can trust the people you are closest to, especially those who are part of your family system. When those who are supposed to love you teach you that love can only come through a sexual experience, you are set up to be used repeatedly as a "sex object."

With each repeated assault your need for love and affirmation grows. In your desperate attempt to be loved, you may seek to fill this need through becoming promiscuous. But each new sexual encounter leaves you feeling more used and less respected and cherished. The void and emptiness in your life grows deeper.

If you were mistreated in childhood, your ability to trust has been disrupted. This breach of trust will have detrimental consequences throughout your lifetime, affecting every decision and relationship you encounter.

Trusting means taking the risk of becoming vulnerable to another human being. It requires emotionally connecting with and becoming involved in another person's life. The inability to trust makes relationship commitments threatening because you fear being used and betrayed again.

Learning to trust will be difficult. After spending time getting to know someone, you have to risk sharing your life with him. Boundaries must be in place in order for you to feel safe enough to reveal the painful experiences from the past that might create problems in your relationship. As you disclose your mistreatment, you develop a more intimate connection with him. The walls that have kept you emotionally detached and alone are slowly removed, and the healing of old wounds begins to take place.

Mind Control

Many times, a perpetrator begins his physical assault by gaining access to the victim's mind. The most power you will ever have is to take control of your mind. You can't afford to let your abuser have access to your most powerful "weapon" as you fight for your very life. You have to exercise authority over your thinking and speaking.

Words have the power to either build us up or destroy us. "Death and life are in the power of the tongue," says Proverbs 18:21 (NASB). As the verbal attacks and comments become more humiliating, your ability to protect yourself and establish boundaries is stripped away. You cannot remain in this destructive situation. Your survival depends on being freed from this disparaging situation.

DEPRESSION

Depression is rarely the result of a single factor. All of us have social, emotional, developmental, genetic, and physiological factors that influence our susceptibility to depression.[16] Biochemical changes are sometimes at the root of depression. A person's physical and emotional realms are strongly connected. A difficulty in one area can trigger problems in the other.

Depression is commonly associated with loss, either tangible or intangible. Intangible losses—loss of trust, innocence, dignity, integrity, and power—inflict the greatest degree of pain.

Most people's lives are filled with changes. Change is always stressful to some degree—even good changes such as getting married, having children, or buying a house. Negative changes such as death, divorce, or losing a job are even more stressful. When too many changes happen in a short period of time, some level of depression may occur.

People who were physically or emotionally abused in childhood tend to have exaggerated physiological responses

---

[16] Les Carter, Ph.D., and Frank Minrith, M.D., *The Freedom from Depression Workbook* (Thomas Nelson Publishers, Nashville, TN, 1995).

to stressful events. Traumatic experiences have a profound effect on the brain's response to stress.[17]

Both women and men experience a plethora of stressful emotions when they suffer abuse. But men have an additional problem because they are taught by society to repress and deny their feelings in order to avoid being stereotyped as weak and feminine. Emotions that women are encouraged to express are seen as signs of frailty in men. But keeping feelings bottled up inside only increases a person's stress level. When emotions are turned inward, they translate into sensations of powerlessness, vulnerability, confusion, guilt, shame, fear, and depression.

When an abused child grows up to become a depressed adult, the cycle of abuse continues. Because a child's identity is closely linked to that of his mother and father, a depressed parent is a threat to a child's personal identity.

A depressed parent tends to isolate herself; she is not available to help her child with homework, activities, friends, or family issues. Since the mother cannot meet her own needs, much less the needs of her child, the child is forced to abandon his childhood and assume the role of caretaker. As a result, the child emerges into adulthood with unmet needs, which create pain and insecurities as he unsuccessfully attempts to fill this void.

Justin, age twenty-six, and Marcie, age twenty-four, had been married for four years when he filed for divorce because of Marcie's controlling and manipulative behavior. Whenever Justin was at home, he claimed, Marcie constantly demanded his time and attention. He couldn't stand having to report his every thought and action to her. She denied being a controller and described her actions as ways of caring for him.

---

[17]   Erica Goode, "Childhood Abuse and Adult Stress," *New York Times*, 2 August 2000.

Marcie often took extended breaks from her job to go to the dental lab where Justin worked. When he had to go out of town for work-related conferences, Marcie always insisted on going with him. She said she just wanted to make sure her husband was taken care of, and she felt unfulfilled and alone when she was not with him.

Justin came from a family where individuals' needs were appropriately met and the family unit maintained a healthy atmosphere in which each member was encouraged to be caring and secure. Marcie was raised in a single-parent home, and her most prevailing memories involved her mother being depressed and unable to care for her.

Marcie was forced into the role of primary caretaker at a very young age. Due to severe depression, her mother spent most of her days in bed while Marcie prepared meals and tended to household chores and responsibilities. The young child comforted her mother during times of loneliness, illness, and emotional outbursts. Marcie never felt safe disclosing her personal needs because she wanted to avoid creating more worry and depression in her mother's life.

As an adult, Marcie sought to have all of her unmet childhood needs fulfilled through her husband. Justin loved his wife, but after four years of constant stress, he started isolating himself from her. He could no longer cope with what he described as his emotional overload.

I explained to Marcie that Justin could be her friend, husband, and lover, but he could never be her mother or absentee father. This was an unrealistic expectation that would be impossible to achieve.

After explaining the dynamics that were taking place in the relationship, Justin agreed to stop the divorce proceedings and be more attentive to his wife. Marcie agreed to fulfill her unmet childhood needs by learning to re-parent herself.

As Marcie worked through her issues in counseling, her insecurities, anxieties, and fears subsided. Justin again felt drawn to his wife as he saw her personal strengths emerge and their relationship flourish.

Like Marcie, victims of abuse who were raised in out-of-control environments know no other lifestyle, and they may refuse to let go of the person they believe will meet all their needs and fulfill their dreams. Often, a woman will stay with her husband until his violence is directed toward the children. Sadly, by this time, the children have already suffered emotional, psychological, and sometimes physical damage that has lifelong detrimental effects.

Children should not have to suffer the consequences of their parents' or other adults' poor choices. If you choose not to leave your environment of violence, love your children enough to put them in a place of safety—perhaps with family, friends, or Child Protective Services.

CONTROLLING BEHAVIORS

Marcie's case is not unusual. A controlling person will seek to implant her attitudes and ideas into the mind of her victim. The controller is confident that if the other person thinks the same way she does, he will behave like she does. Then there will be no need to control him. When this does not work (and it never does), the controller develops a high level of insecurity, which drives her to become even more possessive.

Possessive people cling desperately to the things and people that convince them of their self-worth. The paradox is that clinging to something usually results in losing it. Possessiveness fosters jealousy and jealousy destroys what it claims to love.

It is difficult to act in a truly loving manner if you are afraid of losing the object of your affection. You focus your time and energy on receiving love rather than giving it. You then destroy the object of your possessiveness and destroy yourself in the process.

The only way to stop being possessive is to take care of yourself. Don't expect other people to fulfill all your needs. Try to do for yourself what you've been relying on others to do for you. This may sound terrifying if your worth has been focused externally.

God has given each of us everything we need to live our lives. However, we must nurture and develop our self-worth. We must take responsibility for the success of our lives.

There is a wonderful irony here: The less possessive you are, the more loved you will be. The less you need others, the more they will want to be around you. Secure people, those with a healthy self-esteem, don't have the time or energy to be possessive. They're too busy and content to wait for someone else to meet their needs for them.[18]

ANXIETY AND/OR FEAR

Anxiety is defined as "apprehension, tension, or uneasiness from anticipation of danger, the source of which is largely unknown or unrecognized." This is different from fear, which is "the emotional response to a consciously recognized and usually external threat or danger." Anxiety becomes self-destructive "when it interferes with effectiveness in living, achievement of desired goals or satisfaction, or reasonable emotional comfort."[19]

---

[18] Susanna McMahon, Ph.D., *The Portable Therapist* (Dell Publishing, Bantam Doubleday, Dell Publishing Group, Inc., New York, NY, 1994).

[19] John A. Talbott, M.D., Robert E. Hales, M.D., and Stuart C. Yudofoshy, M.D., eds., *The American Psychiatric Press: Textbook of Psychiatry* (American Psychiatric Press, Inc., First Edition, 1988).

Victims of abuse live with constant anxiety and fear. Because your ability to trust has been shattered, you become hyper-vigilant in your desire to escape further attacks. Every new contact is seen as a potential intruder. You spend your life looking over your shoulder in anticipation of another brutal attack. Your search for safety and security never ends. You will carry anxiety, fear, and stress for several years after the abusive incident—perhaps for your entire lifetime.

Breaking the cycle is difficult because you constantly re-experience the trauma through repeated nightmares, flashbacks, or other occurrences that trigger past memories, feelings, and sensations.

If the degree of fear becomes too intense, you may experience:

- panic attacks
- nervousness
- shortness of breath
- insomnia
- high blood pressure
- rapid heart rate
- inability to concentrate
- uncontrollable crying
- irritability
- excessive worry
- diarrhea/constipation
- muscle tension.

When these sensations become unbearable, you may try to numb yourself psychologically by distancing yourself from life. Unfortunately, this leads to feeling detached and alone, which increases your level of anxiety. Left uncontrolled and untreated, this fear will eventually reach the point where it significantly interferes with your ability to carry out your daily activities.

Since anxiety has the potential to cause dangerous changes in the human body, you should consider a consultation with a physician if the condition persists for several weeks or months. Medical monitoring and/or medication may be necessary for a period of time until the crisis period subsides.

In the long run, the only cure for real fear is to remove the cause of the fear—in this case, the abusive situation. As for anxiety—where you become consumed with apprehension because you are anticipating the possibility of danger—the best solutions are to talk openly with someone about your concerns, provide as safe an environment as possible for yourself, and make a conscious effort to turn your worries over to God. He can provide peace and calm, in spite of your circumstances, as you rest in His love.

BOUNDARY ISSUES

Victims of abuse have a difficult time establishing and maintaining boundaries. Through defining their own personal space, they can gain a sense of identity and power that allows for protection and individual growth.

"Boundaries define a person's physical and emotional areas that should be entered only with his or her permission. A boundary is an imaginary line that separates your space from someone else's . . . The concept of boundaries includes that of personal limits, which means you don't push yourself further or longer than you can comfortably go. You may have gone beyond your personal limits if you find yourself frustrated, depressed, angry, or frightened. Any of these reactions could indicate that you have reached your limit for the time being and should take a break from whatever you are doing. Pay attention to your feelings. Do not force your-self to continue an activity that makes you feel bad."[20]

Setting boundaries means not allowing people to touch you when you don't want to be touched, forcing you into conversations when you don't feel like talking, or attempting to control or manipulate your way of thinking or acting.

Respecting boundaries means the other person respects you as an individual, encourages you, and allows you to achieve your goals and dreams.

Boundaries vary depending on the circumstance and the needs of the person involved. Ongoing defining of bound-aries is critical to the success of any relationship. This can be accomplished with both verbal and nonverbal messages.

"Boundaries protect us. But they don't keep us distant and separated from people. Just the opposite. They provide the foundation for a sound, healthy intimacy. A relationship requires two people who are relating to each other. Lacking awareness of our inner world, we remain enmeshed, not inti-mate. We fuse with the other's universe of feelings, wants and desires. Losing sight of our own inner life, we may later feel resentful because we have not been true to ourselves."[21]

When your identity becomes confused by the chaos sur-rounding you, setting and maintaining boundaries becomes impossible. In order to enjoy healthy relationships, you must possess the self-confidence to be assertive and set limits with those who attempt to become too entangled in your person-al life. Self-assurance begins by choosing to believe in yourself enough to avoid environments and people who will abuse you. You must love yourself in spite of how others view or treat you.

---

[20]   Barbara Bean and Shari Bennett, *The Me Nobody Knows: A Guide for Teen Survivors* (Lexington Books, 1993).

[21]   Charles L. Whitfield, M.D., *Boundaries and Relationships: Knowing, Protecting and Enjoying the Self* (Health Communications, Inc., xix, 1993).

GUILT AND/OR SHAME

Guilt results when you feel you have done something wrong, something that goes against your moral code. Shame results from what someone else has done to you. Both feelings can leave you believing you are "bad" and therefore unworthy of support from others. You feel so humiliated and embarrassed that you don't want anyone to know what has happened to you. You don't think you deserve anyone's investment of time or emotional energy.

Undeserved guilt and shame may cause you to isolate yourself from the very people who can provide the assistance you need and deserve. Revealing the details of a traumatic experience, even to a trusted friend or family member, can help simply by getting the awful secret out into the open.

By sharing the details of your abuse with others, you give them the opportunity to show you unconditional love and acceptance. Through their love, you will begin to see yourself as worthy of being loved. The extraordinary effort that you have used to conceal your abuse can now be redirected toward healing. You can find hope for the future.

Guilt can paralyze you mentally and emotionally, leaving you feeling unworthy of accomplishing or receiving anything good. This sense of guilt leaves you open to further abusive relationships because you feel you deserve to be punished for your past.

One of the most common reasons sexual abuse victims experience confusion, guilt, and shame is that their bodies responded sensually to the touch of their abuser. They may have been lonely and enjoyed the physical closeness that was missing in their life.

Once a person has been touched inappropriately, she is no longer the same. All of her instincts for survival and protection are snatched away. She is left with a haunting guilt and shame that remains with her for a lifetime.

You may feel guilty because you didn't say no, even though you were powerless to do so at the time. Many times victims of abuse are so terrified they become paralyzed mentally, emotionally, and physically. They are literally unable to move or speak. They become lifeless, incapable of escaping the horrific experience that is taking place. It is important to realize that you had no control over the offense committed against you. You were a victim. You were powerless to change or stop the abuse.

SENSE OF POWERLESSNESS

When an unexpected terrifying event happens, you enter a stage of shock that leaves you incapable of functioning as a confident human being. Your identity becomes confused, and you may emotionally regress to an earlier time when life was safe and others made all your decisions.

A similar sense of powerlessness results when subtle violations occur over a period of time. Repeated incidents of abuse may have left you feeling you had no right to make decisions, set limits, establish boundaries, express opinions, or see yourself as a worthy individual. Each assault, whether verbal or physical, makes you more susceptible to repeated victimization. The only choice you may see is to obey the orders of others, even when those orders result in further abuse.

The goal of the abuser is to make you feel powerless and dependent on him. He dominates and controls conversations, so you become confused and unable to see what is happening to you. He convinces you that you are stupid and incapable of interpreting life. He demands sex often, making you feel you have no right to refuse. He convinces you that you do not have control over your own body.

As the abuser's mental trap intensifies, you gradually become unable to see anything wrong with his actions.

He convinces you that his behavior is normal, and that if you're uncomfortable, that's because you have unresolved issues and problems. You are the one who is "abnormal."

The perpetrator may also limit your financial and material resources so you cannot move out and become independent. If he sees you gaining any sort of independence, he becomes angry and inflicts further abuse. He may express his wrath by destroying personal possessions of yours, especially ones that give you a sense of pride in yourself. Pride could lead to independence, which would be a threat to him. If you become self-reliant, he will be powerless: a state in which he cannot survive.

If he senses that he is beginning to lose control, he may implement strategies to manipulate and threaten you. One of the most successful ways of doing this is to seek your forgiveness for his inappropriate behavior. He promises he will never hurt you again. Like a helpless child who desperately needs to be loved, you fall back under his control. And the cycle continues.

An abused child will often pick up the message that there are two kinds of people: abusers and victims. It is clear where the power lies—only abusers are permitted to express their feelings. Angry responses by the child usually provoke further abuse. Crying is perceived as a weakness, which leads to more victimization. The abused child draws the logical conclusion that to be powerful, he must become an abuser.[22]

INTIMACY PROBLEMS

For two people to experience true intimacy, their relationship must include honesty, sharing, caring, trust, love, communication, commitment, respect, and shared responsibilities. They need to remove their masks and facades, tear

---

[22] Mike Lew, *Victims No Longer: Men Recovering from Incest and Other Sexual Child Abuse* (Harper Collins Publishers, Inc., New York, NY, 1990).

down emotional walls, and say to each other, "This is what I feel, think, hope, and desire. These are my fears, goals, and dreams. Please be a part of my real world and know me for who I truly am."

This kind of intimacy allows both people in a relationship to experience the deep satisfaction of complete personal disclosure. When we are in an intimate relationship, we are able to have our needs met and to feel love and acceptance.

Intimacy does not mean that two people become so interconnected that they lose their ability to live as individuals. On the contrary, it allows them to experience life in many meaningful ways. They can interpret the events in their lives from their own perspective, without fear of rejection or condemnation. They can eagerly look forward to sharing and exchanging new insights.

Individuals who have experienced violence and abuse develop barriers that prevent them from forming healthy intimate relationships. These "walls of protection" are controlled by the person who abused you. You are overtaken with fear and distrust. So you live life feeling alone and rejected because *nobody understands your pain*. To hide your insecurities, you attempt to send out bold messages of independence, confidence, and power. But as you withdraw into your world of seclusion, you are seen as cold, distant, and uncaring.

A lack of healthy relationships with people also affects your ability to have an intimate relationship with God. Many times, a victim of abuse cannot trust God because she holds a great deal of anger and bitterness toward Him. You may feel God abandoned you in your time of greatest need, leaving you stranded and helpless. You may have prayed for protection or deliverance countless times, yet the abuse continued. With each additional abusive encounter, the gap between your troubled world and God's perfect heaven widened.

Understandably, you have become confused, perhaps even doubting if God truly exists. Well-meaning believers may try to encourage you by telling you about others whom God protected or rescued. But this only causes you to become more angry, to feel that God must have favorites and that you certainly aren't one of them. This deepens your feelings of insignificance.

Rather than hearing miraculous testimonies of deliverance, you need someone to listen to you and validate your feelings. You want someone to understand your pain. It only makes matters worse if people make condescending remarks or try to convince you to "snap out of it."

When we try to understand the infinite sovereignty of God with our finite minds, there are no simple answers. During times like this, all we can do is pray. It is the Holy Spirit's job to help us understand Him. As we pray and are prayed for by others, God will give us spiritual eyes and ears to see and hear what He has in store for us. Our relationship with God has to be personal in order for Him to work and reveal Himself to us.

If abuse has clouded your view of God, it may be difficult for you to have a rich, meaningful relationship with Him. This cannot occur until you go through the process of healing from the tragedy that has taken place in your life. As you learn to trust, you will be better able to enter into a true, intimate relationship with Jesus Christ.

He lovingly and graciously waits to respond to your pleas for help in much the same way a loving earthly parent does. When a child's life is filled with pain, his parents may want to rush to his side and take the pain away. But no matter how much they may want to help, their ability to do so will be limited by the child's desire to receive their assistance.

God can only work in your life to the extent that you allow Him to. God wants to restore the brokenhearted and set the captives free. "Who redeems your life from the pit; who crowns you with loving kindness and compassion; who satisfies your years with good things, so that your youth is renewed like the eagle" (Psalm 103:4-5 NASB).

You must choose to trust God, even when everything inside you screams that trusting is not safe. You may think you have faith in God, but the real test is taking that step beyond faith and truly trusting Him with the plans He has for your life, even when you can't see what those plans might be. As the writer of Hebrews tells us, "Faith is being sure of what we hope for and certain of what we do not see" (11:1). You can say you have faith that God has the power to do anything, but do you trust Him enough to allow Him to do whatever He chooses for your life?

People who have not suffered abuse find it easier to trust God because their experiences have taught them that trusting is safe. However, you have had your ability to trust stolen from you. You do not possess the necessary foundation on which to build intimate relationships with people or with the Lord. Pray, expressing to God your desire to trust Him. Ask Him to work in your life so you can develop this trust.

THE FUTURE IS UP TO YOU

The abusive experiences in your past have shaped your view of life, the world, and the people around you. These events have determined your understanding of yourself and others. Although your past has been tarnished with pain and suffering, you have a choice. You can allow these hurtful circumstances to result in bitterness, skepticism, and hatred, which will further damage you. Or you can allow them to provide you with a unique level of compassion. You can see the world in a way that those who have not experienced such trauma never will. This insight into the obscurity of abuse can equip you to make a difference in the life of another person and the world around you.

If you choose to work through the process of healing, you will someday be able to help others who have experienced similar devastation. Then, when someone says, *"Nobody understands my pain,"* you can reply, "I've been there. Let me show you how you can get through this."

CHAPTER 3

THE SYMPTOM OF LOW SELF-ESTEEM

The most common symptom of emotional abuse is low self-esteem. A disparaging assessment of personal value leads victims into lives filled with turmoil and anguish. People with low self-esteem can often recall painful incidents in their early home environment. Perhaps you felt criticized and shamed by your parents' inability to show affirming acts of love or by their attempts to control and manipulate your behavior. These childhood experiences set you up to relive old feelings from your past each time you are exposed to disapproval or rejection. Similar comments or situations may seem benign or uneventful to others, but for you they are triggers for intense pain and grief.

The most important people in a child's life are his or her parents. Your parents help to lay the basic foundation of core beliefs for you to feel loved, significant, and worthy as a human being. This sense of being valued and loved becomes the primary building block of your self-concept. If you were never validated by your parents, you may have felt that your life was void of meaning or direction. In an attempt to survive, you began a long, arduous journey that left you vulnerable to further abuse and neglect.

A healthy self-esteem is foundational to emotional/psychological success. Many people attempt to find happiness through the accumulation of social status, wealth, or material possessions. This kind of happiness, if achieved at all, is short lived. No matter how much you have, financial achievements are never enough. The emotional void remains. Your only hope is to triumph over the lingering recollections of the past.

Your self-concept will directly determine the outcome of your life. Proverbs 23:7 reveals, "For as he [a man] thinketh in his heart, so is he" (KJV).

Self-esteem can best be described as an individual's personal assessment of himself, the value he places on his life. Your ability to love, respect, and honor yourself is dependent upon the degree of approval you have for yourself. We all view our life decisions through the perception of our self-image and past experiences. Self-esteem plays a major role in determining our peer groups, academic achievements, careers, relationships, and even our concept of God.

RECOVERING FROM A LOW SELF-ESTEEM

Phil was one of four children born into a family that placed high value on intelligence and academic success. Both his mother and his father had graduated from prestigious universities summa cum laude and were highly respected by friends and acquaintances. Phil and his siblings were expected to excel in all areas of life, especially in academia. For his brothers and sisters, learning appeared easy, requiring very little time or effort. But for Phil, the classroom was a major challenge that became a constant source of defeat. His mother and father berated him when he failed and never praised his efforts or successes. They seemed to see only his failures.

Through elementary and high school, Phil managed to pass all of his classes and was ecstatic when he received a letter of acceptance into a community college. But a community college was unacceptable to his parents, who considered anything other than a major university an embarrassment to the family reputation.

Phil's father refused to pay for tuition at the community college. He continued his verbal attacks, accusing his son of being lazy, stupid, and dumb. He told Phil he would never amount to anything. Eventually, Phil's parents convinced him that he was incapable of being successful.

With a crushed spirit and low self-esteem, Phil left home and began a life in which alcohol and drugs compensated for the lack of approval from his parents.

As the result of a suicide attempt at the age of twenty, Phil was admitted into the psychiatric unit of a local hospital. After a battery of tests and inpatient therapy, Phil was diagnosed with a learning disorder and severe depression due to his parents' disapproval and rejection.

Over the next twelve months, he underwent extensive Christian counseling. With the help of prescribed medication, he was able to concentrate and stay focused on tasks. His desire for drugs and alcohol ceased. Phil became a new creation in Christ, which allowed him to forgive and reconcile with his parents, even though they were never willing to accept responsibility for the part they played in his failure.

Today, Phil is a college graduate. He owns and operates his own computer business. He also enjoys motivational speaking, sharing with others that his success in life comes from knowing who he is in Christ and being determined to find answers to his problems. He considers all of his business accomplishments as blessings from God.

Low self-esteem casts dark shadows over the lives of individuals in pain. These people are unable to see beyond their past failures and mistakes. "A poor self-image is the magnifying glass that can transform a trivial mistake or an imperfection into an overwhelming symbol of personal defeat."[23]

---

23   David Burns, M.D., *Feeling Good* (William Morrow and Company, Inc., New York, NY, 1980).

If you see yourself as a failure, unlovable and unworthy, you will be unable to receive Christ's love and redemption for sin. Until you truly know Him through a spiritual rebirth into the kingdom of God, the message of His love will fall on deaf ears. You may believe He loves people and died for them, but you will not be able to personalize this belief until you understand how much God loves you.

You may be tempted to hide your insecurities and fears by making yourself appear stronger than you really are. You say all the right things, but deep inside you doubt the motives of the people who are trying to support you. You may even doubt God.

Once you begin to accept love and help from others, you will learn how to love yourself. This, in turn, can help you experience the love of God.

God offers true, lasting peace. Christ reassures the one who believes in Him, "I have told you these things, so that in me you may have peace. In this world you will have trouble. But take heart! I have overcome the world" (John 16:33).

Satan fights hardest to gain strongholds in our minds and emotions. He can easily do so if we do not guard ourselves with spiritual truth from the Word of God. Because our feelings can be so powerful, our minds can become confused and disillusioned, leaving us with a sense of hopelessness, despair, and low self-esteem.

God is the only everlasting Prince of Peace, and He alone can bring about true contentment and happiness. He loves you and desires good things for your life. He loved you so much that He died for you. Your value is based on His pure and unconditional love for you.

If you fall into the world system that says your worth is dependent upon the love of others, money, material possessions, prestige, or reputation, you are setting yourself up for failure and heartache. If you allow others to determine how you feel about yourself, your hurt and disappointment will lead to distress and depression. These outside forces will always be in control of you and your destiny.

In reality, no one can make you feel anything without your permission to do so. You must constantly be on guard to prevent destructive words, actions, and comments from taking root in your mind. You can choose to feel good about yourself and reject messages that will destroy your self-esteem. Remember, the only control you have is self-control, which is the very thing that will determine how others affect you.

People often live with the false belief that they can and should obtain everyone's approval, love, and acceptance. With this mind-set, you are doomed for a life filled with unrealistic expectations and disappointments. No one can ever have complete approval and acceptance from everyone.

BUILDING A HEALTHY SELF-ESTEEM

Healing begins with a decision to incorporate core beliefs that enable you to see yourself as God does.

The moment you accept Jesus Christ as your personal Savior, you receive the power to love yourself. Although abuse is still part of your past, it no longer controls you because you have become a new creation in Him (2 Corinthians 5:17 NLT). All of your guilt, shame, insecurities, and pain can be healed and taken away. The old life is gone. A new life has begun! Every time your past tries to creep back in, you can remind yourself that you are a new person in Christ and walk in freedom and tranquility.

As you work through your past and live a Christ-centered life, the Holy Spirit develops within you a healthy self-concept that is manifested as the fruit of the Spirit. Galatians 5:22 says, "The fruit of the Spirit is love, joy, peace, patience, kindness, goodness, faithfulness, gentleness and self-control." Through His power you can have victory over the obstacles in your life.

Your greatest challenge should be to find God's will for your life. This process starts by desiring a close bond with Him. We become more like Christ when we emulate His character and His holiness.

To do this we must take on the mind of Christ. The apostle Paul said, "Do not conform any longer to the pattern of this world, but be transformed by the renewing of your mind. Then you will be able to test and approve what God's will is—his good, pleasing and perfect will" (Romans 12:2).

Once you decide to heal, you may believe that you should just be able to *get over it.* But recovery is not that easy. The healing process takes time. As you overcome your past, you may occasionally become disappointed and view yourself as weak, or a failure.

If you are a Christian, you may further berate yourself for your inability to trust God. This misconception is sometimes reinforced by well-meaning Christians. Because they lack understanding of the emotional and physical trauma you have gone through, they may further traumatize you with comments such as "Just let it go" or "You're not trusting God enough."

Before people can support you in recovery, they must choose to view your life experiences through your eyes and emotions instead of theirs. No one can be expected to truly understand something he has never experienced. But if people are willing to listen, you can help them gain insight and knowledge into your world.

As you live in God's will over time you can have the confidence to stand against the enemy, who desires to overtake and destroy you. As you grow in Christ you will become more aware of Satan's subtle attacks. "For our struggle is not against flesh and blood, but against the rulers, against the authorities, against the powers of this dark world and against the spiritual forces of evil in the heavenly realms" (Ephesians 6:12).

BUILDING SELF-ESTEEM IN OTHERS

To help build up those we care about, we must place value on them by listening to, acknowledging, and accepting their feelings and their unique individuality. They must receive respect, honor, and praise not only for their accomplishments but for their efforts as well.

Failure is not the inability to accomplish certain goals, but allowing fear to keep us from trying to reach them. Success is not about finishing in first place. It is about gaining knowledge and personal satisfaction for our efforts.

Many people who are beautiful and intelligent harbor such low self-esteem that they become paralyzed with fear. Ironically, this fear causes them to avoid taking the risks required to accomplish the very tasks that would boost their self-confidence.

MY OWN STRUGGLE WITH SELF-ESTEEM

In 1985, my immune system was almost completely destroyed due to a series of exposures to toxic chemicals. I became severely allergic to everything in the world: perfume, hair spray, makeup, deodorant, shampoo, lotions, mold, trees, grass, dust, plastic, paper and ink, synthetic material, dyes, and essentially all foods . . . basically, everything I could touch, taste, or smell.

The doctors held little hope. For almost a year, I lived in total isolation in my home. For four more years, my health remained unstable. I wanted to die, thinking that would be better for everyone involved.

During this time, my physical appearance changed dramatically. My long, thick, shiny brown hair became thin, sparse, brittle, and dull. My healthy body quickly deteriorated to a state of emaciation. My eyes, which used to dance with joy and laughter, were hollow and sad.

In addition, much of my identity was based on my position as a school nurse. One of the most difficult days of my life was when I had to resign from that job because I couldn't carry out my responsibilities.

But nothing compares to the loss I felt when I could no longer experience the joys and privileges of being a wife and mother. I detested losing the active role I had always played in my husband and children's lives.

I lived in frustration because no matter how hard I tried to explain to people what I was going through, words were inadequate. My life was bizarre. *And nobody understood my pain.*

After many months of tears, fear, aggravation, disappointment, and anger—fighting a battle I had no hope of winning—I became exhausted and lifeless. I finally came to the realization that being in God's will and accepting who I was in Him were far more important than looking a particular way or carrying out certain roles, even those fulfilling and important roles of wife and mother.

When I got on my knees at three o'clock one morning and cried out to the Lord in my hopeless state, I began to understand what true peace, happiness, and significance were all about. Even if I never recovered from my illness, I could have peace and a sense of value simply by focusing on how much God loved me and knowing that He had a plan for my life. I began seeking Him more desperately than I ever had before.

The prayer that changed my life was "Lord, even if I am never healed, if I never leave this isolation room, I want to know You like I have never known You before." I knew that once I accepted God's will for my life, I would be content and accept my condition and my future, whatever they might be.

The world's system for determining a person's self-worth no longer mattered to me. I knew who I was in Christ. Because of this, I found purpose and meaning in my life.

After years of struggle and determination, leaning on the Lord and trusting Him unreservedly, I regained my health through a series of both natural and supernatural events. Though my toxic exposures had threatened to destroy me, by the power of God I was able to live a normal, healthy life again.

You can experience God's freedom and power in your life too.

CHAPTER 4

THE SYMPTOM OF ADDICTION

 motionally damaged people often suffer from addictions to one or more of the following:

- Alcohol and/or Drugs

- The Internet

- Gambling

- Sex

In an attempt to escape the reality of your abusive past (and/or present), you may turn to things you hope will take away your pain. Even inherently good things like sex, or innocuous activities such as surfing the Internet, can become self-destructive if misused.

How can you distinguish between a passion and an addiction? A passion adds value to your life; an addiction takes away value. Unfortunately, when that line is crossed, the addict is often the last to know.

The essence of all addictions is the addict's powerlessness over his compulsive behavior. You may wish to stop, yet repeatedly fail to do so. The dysfunction of your life is seen in the consequences you suffer: loss of relationships, difficulties with work, health issues, legal problems, financial trouble, despair, and/or a loss of interest in activities not related to the addiction.

ALCOHOL/DRUGS

People who were abused as children are more likely to become addicted to alcohol or drugs as adults. Tragically, alcoholics and drug addicts are more likely to abuse their children. Without intervention, the cycle can be unending.[24] Fifty to 80 percent of all child-abuse cases substantiated by Child Protective Services involve some degree of substance abuse by the child's parents.[25] Children in alcohol-abusing families are nearly four times more likely to be maltreated, almost five times more likely to be physically neglected, and ten times more likely to be emotionally neglected than children in non-alcohol-abusing families.[26]

Terry was a slim, handsome, fifty-four-year-old banker. He arrived for counseling at my clinic dressed in a dark tailored suit, white dress shirt, and designer tie.

He told me his first wife divorced him because he was an alcoholic and a workaholic. Many nights he came home around ten o'clock after having worked a fourteen-hour day.

Terry's second wife constantly threatened to leave him due to his obsessive work schedule, his habitual drinking, and his emotional detachment from the family. Neither of his wives knew he had any addictions prior to their marriage because Terry only drank and used drugs when he was alone.

As I worked with Terry, I discovered that his mother was an alcoholic who frequently used illegal drugs. She was also

---

[24]   Elaine M. Johnson, Ph.D., National Clearinghouse for Alcohol and Drug Information, Rockville, MD, October 1995 (info@health.org).

[25]   "A Report on Child Maltreatment in Alcohol-Abusing Families," U.S. Department of Health and Human Services, National Center on Child Abuse and Neglect, Washington, DC: Government Printing Office, 1993.

[26]   "A Report on Child Maltreatment in Alcohol-Abusing Families," U.S. Department of Health and Human Services, National Center on Child Abuse and Neglect, Washington, DC: Government Printing Office, 1993.

a victim of childhood sexual abuse. She was married for seven years to Terry's father, who was also an alcoholic. Her drunken husband often raped her at night. He made no attempts to form any kind of relationship with his son.

When Terry was four years old, his mother began sleeping with him. As she slipped into bed with him, she would fondle him and say, "Daddy hurt me, so now you have to make me feel good." She then instructed young Terry in how to fondle her.

As he grew older, these childhood experiences led Terry to seek escape in alcohol and drugs as he tried to cope with the guilt, shame, and loneliness of his life. At age twelve, he began sneaking alcohol from his mother's kitchen pantry. By age sixteen he was an alcoholic and smoked marijuana on a regular basis.

When Terry came to see me, I immediately recommended that he start attending Alcoholics Anonymous meetings. After extensive counseling and continual participation in AA, he was able to overcome his addictions to alcohol and drugs. In time, Terry confronted his mother and father to work through issues related to his childhood abuse. He also saved his second marriage.

Today Terry is a strong advocate for child safety and addiction recovery. He serves on several committees that support programs to prevent abuse and facilitate healing for people who are addicted.

THE INTERNET

The Internet can be a valuable tool, an entertaining amusement, or a destructive addiction. When "surfing" becomes an obsession, family and friends can suffer great loss from the addict's activity. Broken marriages, lost jobs, failing school grades, and missed meals are some of the consequences of people who become addicted to the Internet.

If you are an Internet addict, you have formed deep emotional attachments to online friends and activities. You enjoy those aspects of the Internet that allow you to meet, socialize, and exchange ideas with new people through interactive applications such as chatting, online games, or newsgroups. These virtual communities offer both an escape from reality and a means to fulfill unmet emotional and psychological needs.

On the Internet, you can conceal your name, age, occupation, appearance—even your gender—from anyone you encounter online. If you are lonely and insecure in real-life situations, you may take advantage of this freedom to pour out your strongest feelings, darkest secrets, and deepest desires. This leads to the illusion of intimacy. However, when you eventually realize the severe limitations of relying on a faceless community for the love and caring that can only come from real people, you will experience severe disappointment and pain.[27]

The Internet can trap you into a world of fantasy. You wind up lying to yourself and others. And you miss the opportunity to heal because you never face your abusive past. As a result, you continue your aimless journey through life, constantly searching for a means to fill the void.

GAMBLING

Victims of abuse frequently become compulsive, which leads them to become risk takers. They feel a significant portion of their life was stolen from them, so they want to take something away from others. Gambling offers these victims a feeling of power.

---

[27] K. S. Young, "What Makes On-line-Usage Stimulating? Potential explanations for pathological Internet use," *Symposia* presented at the 105th annual meeting of the American Psychological Association, August 15, 1997, Chicago, IL.

For non-addicts, money spent on gambling does not affect family finances because it is set aside for entertainment. But for problem gamblers, excessive spending creates serious consequences for the family. Often it means that bills don't get paid, utilities are cut off, and the grocery money dwindles. Pathological gamblers sometimes finance their habit with money from welfare checks or the sale of personal items.

A study published in the International Journal of Addictions reported a high correlation between pathological gambling and a history of emotional trauma. It theorized that the immediate gratification of gambling offers a "temporary respite in the insatiable quest for self-affirmation."[28]

The "temporary respite" of gambling leaves the abused person demanding attention and approval from others. This places tremendous stress on the spouse and children. Although compulsive gamblers tend to be less violent than the general population, their mates tend to be more violent. This suggests that pathological gamblers may provoke reactive violence in their spouses.[29]

Children of pathological gamblers are twice as likely to attempt suicide, receive lower grades in school, and have higher rates of substance abuse.[30] Studies suggest that children of pathological gamblers are more likely to have

---

[28]   J. I. Taber, R. A. McCormick, and I. F. Ramirez, "The Prevalence and Impact of Major Life Stressors among Pathological Gamblers," *The International Journal of the Addictions*, 1987, 22(1), 71-79.

[29]   H. Lesieur, "Family Issues and Compulsive Gambling," *Report on Pathological Gambling in New Jersey*, Governor's Advisory Commission on Gambling, 1988, 124.

[30]   D. F. Jacobs, et. al., "Children of Problem Gamblers," *Journal of Gaming Behavior*, V:4, 1989, 261-268.

gambling problems themselves than children whose parents do not have gambling problems.[31]

SEX

God created sex to be enjoyed by two people involved in a life-long commitment known as marriage. In His divine wisdom, He intended shared sexual experiences to be the most private part of a relationship—so intimate that no other human being has the privilege of sharing in it. It is this intimacy that allows a married couple to grow together as they build a lifetime of trust, respect, honor, and pleasure.

Outside these parameters, however, sexual involvement has lasting, damaging effects. Society and the entertainment media purport that sex before or outside marriage is a personal choice, wholesome and healthy as long as it is performed between two consenting adults. But casual attitudes about sex can lead to all manner of self-esteem, trust, and commitment issues. When taken to the extreme, sex can become a tool to manipulate the other person in a relationship.

Because sex can be such an exciting and pleasurable experience, you may be misled into believing that the feelings it creates are love. Marriages based on sex fail because the true ingredients of love are missing.

Sexual addiction manifests itself in various ways, including *promiscuity, pornography,* and *homosexuality.*

Promiscuity

Abuse has destroyed your self-esteem. It has made you feel unlovable, yet your desire to be loved continues. In an attempt to fill this void, you may look for love in all the wrong places and in all the wrong ways.

You may become promiscuous, thinking that sex will provide the love you crave. When it doesn't, you may not realize

---

[31] H. Lesieur and R. Klein, "Pathological Gambling among High School Students," Addictive Behaviors, 1987, 129-135.

THE SYMPTOM OF ADDICTION

that the fault lies not with the sexual partner you have chosen, but with your method of equating sex with love. Therefore, you constantly seek new sexual partners. With each new partner, your sense of value plummets further and your desire for sexual encounters becomes stronger.

Sexual addiction is probably the most hidden of all obsessions. Even those who recognize they are addicted to sex usually deny that it has any negative effect on their lives.

Exodus International, an organization that ministers to people struggling with sexual issues, states, "Sexual activity usually covers deep wounds. Once activity stops, the 'painkiller' of sex wears off and underlying emotional pain surfaces."[32]

As with other addictions, sex addicts often come from dysfunctional families in which parents were chemically dependent, sexually addicted, abusive, or otherwise emotionally unavailable.

Dr. Patrick Carnes, a leading authority on sexual addiction, conducted a survey of almost 900 adult sex addicts and found that 82 percent of these people were sexually abused during their childhood.[33]

In a survey of recovering sex addicts, only 20 percent said their parents had no addiction. In 40 percent of the families, at least one parent was chemically dependent. One or both parents were sex addicts in 36 percent. In 33 percent, at least one parent had an eating disorder. In 7 percent, one parent was a compulsive gambler. [34]

Children who are sexually abused grow up fearing sex, confusing sex with love, or believing that the only way to

---

32   www.ExodusNorthAmerica.org

33   P. J. Carnes, *Don't Call It Love: Recovery From Sexual Addiction* (Bantam Books, New York, 1991), 42-4.

34   J. P. Schneider and B. Schneider, *Sex, Lies, and Forgiveness: Couples Speaking Out on Healing from Sex Addiction* (Hazelden Educational Materials, Center City, MN, 1991).

relate to others is sexually. Some grow up to become perpetrators of sexual abuse themselves.

Like chemical dependency, sexual addiction is a family disease. Spouses of sex addicts, or "co-addicts," usually grew up in a dysfunctional family where they were sexually abused and thus have fear or confusion about sex. They may believe that no one could love them for themselves, that they can control others, or that sex is the most important sign of love.

Co-addicts tend to be attracted to individuals who are needy, which describes most addicts. They usually fear abandonment, cannot imagine life without their partners, and are willing to accept behaviors that healthier persons find unacceptable. In a survey of recovering co-addicts, 66 percent said they had participated in sexual activities they found uncomfortable. These included viewing pornography, swapping sexual partners, and having sex in public places.[35]

Pornography

Obsession with pornography isn't a public addiction, like alcoholism or drug abuse, but a private, secret thing. Friends and family members rarely know when their loved ones are addicted.

Pornography addicts come from all walks of life, all races and creeds. They may be Christian, Jewish, or atheist; attractive or homely; single or married; fathers or mothers.

Pornography is destructive for both the viewer and the person being viewed. Marriages are dissolved, homes are broken, individuals lose their dignity and self-respect.

---

[35] J. P. Schneider, *Back from Betrayal: Recovering from His Affairs* (Harper/Hazelden, San Francisco, 1988), 26-35.

The Victims of Pornography Web site[36] reports the following statistics:

- Among 932 sex addicts, 90 percent of men and 77 percent of women reported pornography as significant to their addictions. The study also revealed that two common causes of sexually addictive behavior are childhood sexual abuse and frequent pornography accompanied by masturbation.[37]

- Research gathered over the past few decades demonstrates that pornography contributes to sexual assault, including rape and the molestation of children.[38]

- Child molesters often use pornography to seduce their prey, to lower the inhibitions of the victim, and to serve as an instruction manual.[39]

- Of thirty-six serial sex murderers interviewed by the FBI in 1985, 81 percent admitted using pornography.[40]

- 87 percent of girl child molesters and 77 percent of boy child molesters studied admitted to regular use

---

[36] www.victimsofpornography.org/Facts_Figures/Pornography_and_ Violence/pornography_and_violence.htm.

[37] Patrick Carnes, *Don't Call it Love: Recovery from Sexual Addictions* (Bantam Books, 1992).

[38] Pornography Victims Compensation Act of 1992, Senate Comm. on the Judiciary, S. Rep. No. 102-372, 102nd Cong., 2nd Sess. 23 (August 12, 1992).

[39] W. L. Marshall, Ph.D., "Pornography and Sexual Offenders," *Pornography: Research Advances and Policy Considerations* (D. Zillmann & J. Bryant eds., 1989).

[40] Victor Cline, Ph.D., *Pornography Effects: Empirical & Clinical Evidence* (University of Utah, Department of Psychology, 1988), 19.

of hard-core pornography.[41]

• One in three American girls and one in seven boys will be sexually molested by age eighteen.[42]

Pornography pollutes the mind of the viewer and causes his beliefs about sex and love to be tarnished. It degrades sex from a beautiful expression of love to a selfish, empty, demeaning act of lust. For the person forced to participate in this humiliating act, pornography results in exploitation, abuse, and pain.

One of my clients, a fifty-year-old woman named Gail, was considerably overweight when she first came to my office. As she told me her story, I quickly understood the psychological reasons behind her weight problem.

During adolescence, Gail's stepfather regularly viewed pornography. Despite her protests, he often took nude pictures of Gail's petite teenage body. He weighed her every day, to keep her looking as "perfect" as the undressed models he viewed. To monitor what she ate, he measured everything in the refrigerator. He taped the kitchen cabinets shut, marking the tapelines on the cabinet doors so he could determine if she had opened them to get food.

Family members tried to sneak food to Gail when her stepfather was not around. If she gained any weight, he beat her. She became afraid of eating. Hunger pains were far less agonizing than the sexual and physical abuse from her stepfather.

He made her run every day before and after school, running alongside her to set the pace. If she complained or was unable to keep up with him, he made her run barefoot on unpaved roads.

---

41   Dr. William Marshall, "A Report on the Use of Pornography by Sexual Offenders," Ottawa, Canada (for the Federal Department of Justice, 1983).

42   David Finkelhor, Director of the Crimes against Children Research Center, "Answers to Important Questions about the Scope & Nature of Child Sexual Abuse," July 1993, p. 8.

One day Gail's stepfather drove her to a nearby lake. He threatened to put her in a large plastic bag and drop her into the water if she ever told anyone about the abuse. "And if that happens," he assured her, "you won't ever resurface. I'll make sure of that."

When Gail left home to go to college, she immediately started gaining weight. The over-consumption of food brought a sense of control in her life. No longer could her stepfather withhold food from her. No longer could he determine the size and shape of her body. No longer would he or anyone else control her life. The extra pounds made her feel "safe" from exploitation and further abuse. Food brought temporary comfort and pleasure to her pain-filled life.

Gail is presently in counseling, working through the years of anguish and torture she endured as a child.

Homosexuality

Much controversy exists over the subject of homosexuality. There are two opposing views. Some people believe that individuals are born with homosexual tendencies; others declare that homosexuality is a choice. The purpose of this section is not to debate the issue of origin but to show the relationship between abuse, neglect, poor relationships, and homosexuality.

The cover of the August 17, 1998, issue of *Newsweek* magazine showed married couple John and Anne Paulk, self-proclaimed "ex-gays," with the headline "Gay for Life? Going Straight: The Uproar Over Sexual 'Conversion.' " In this issue, Exodus International is quoted as saying, "Boys with absent fathers, girls with absent mothers, get stuck in developmental limbo and seek masculine or feminine fulfillment through sex with members of their own gender."[43]

---

[43] www.ExodusNorthAmerica.org.

Exodus Ministries' Web site sates, "We see such a similarity in personal backgrounds among the men and women who seek our help. There is a pretty uniform picture of poor family dynamics in general, a rift in the father-son or mother-daughter relationship growing up, feelings of being an outsider among one's peers during childhood and adolescence, and instances of sexual abuse/incest."[44]

Marjorie Hopper, director of Another Chance Ministries, a Vancouver-based ex-gay ministry for individuals wanting to come out of the homosexual lifestyle, points out, "Homosexuality is not something you are, but something you do."[45] According to Ms. Hopper, the first step toward freedom from homosexuality is to look at the root causes that may drive a person into a homosexual lifestyle: emotional damage occurring at an early age, a sexual identity deficit, and other personal vulnerabilities such as sexual abuse or 'labeling.' Another Chance Ministries' Web site goes on to report, "When the homosexual impulse is acted on, it increases the sexual, emotional and spiritual brokenness and can lead to this lifestyle."[46]

From May 1989 through April 1990, over one thousand homosexual and bisexual men were interviewed regarding abusive sexual activity during childhood and adolescence. Thirty-seven percent of the participants reported they had been encouraged or forced to have sexual contact before age nineteen with an older or more powerful partner.[47]

---

[44] Ibid.

[45] www.acminc.com.

[46] www.AnotherChance.org.

[47] L. S. Doll, et. al., "Self-Reported Childhood and Adolescent Sexual Abuse among Adult Homosexual Bisexual Men," *Child Abuse and Neglect*, 16, no. 6, 1992, 855-64.

The same is true for pedophiles. "The association between perpetration of sexual abuse and the offender's own victimization as a child has been well documented."[48] A boy who has been raped by a man may develop a belief that he is somewhat feminine, since a male was so attracted to him. As he grows up, the incident of abuse becomes fixed in his mind. Eventually, this disconcerting occurrence may cause him to believe that he is somehow "designed" to receive sexual satisfaction only from someone of his own gender.

In 1 Corinthians 6:9-11, the apostle Paul defines the types of sinners who will not inherit the kingdom of God. This list includes, but is not limited to, those who practice homosexuality. Paul goes on to say, "And that is what some of you were." Some of the people in Corinth had been living homosexual lifestyles. "But you were washed," Paul writes, "you were sanctified, you were justified in the name of the Lord Jesus Christ and by the Spirit of our God." These former homosexuals changed when they came to Christ, just like the thieves, the greedy, the drunkards, the slanderers, and the swindlers in the remainder of Paul's list.

When Hector came to my office for counseling, he reported that he could not remember a single day when he was happy and excited about life. His earliest memory was of playing with a toy pistol and wishing he could kill himself with it. He was five years old at the time.

Hector had other childhood memories, mainly of his cold, distant, and verbally abusive father. Hector became quiet and withdrawn, and he picked up some effeminate mannerisms. Because he was fearful of people, he never joined in activities with other children. They laughed at him and

---

[48] D. M. Greenberg, J. M. Bradford, and S. Curry, "A Comparison of Sexual Victimization in the Childhoods of Pedophiles and Hebephiles," *Journal of Forensic Science* (United States) 38, no. 2, March 1993, 432-36.

called him names, sometimes feminine ones such as "sissy" or "little girl."

As Hector grew up, his depression became more severe. When he was a teenager, he saw a psychiatrist who diagnosed him with clinical depression and prescribed an antidepressant drug, which Hector took for years.

Hector attended college, made good grades, and spent most of his time alone. When he graduated, he worked in cancer research. But loneliness and powerlessness continued to overshadow him.

In an effort to find meaning in his life, Hector volunteered to coach sports activities for boys ages six to twelve. He became involved in the boys' lives, particularly those who lived in single-parent homes and were looking for a father figure. Everybody thought Hector was wonderful, but within a short period of time he began molesting one of the young boys. The exploitation gave him a sense of power and control.

Eventually, the abuse was reported and Hector was placed on probation for ten years. He was listed as a sex offender in the National Sex Offenders Registry.

After several years, Hector met an older man who seemed to love him. He started living with this man, believing they had an ideal relationship. However, the man turned out to be just like Hector's father—controlling, detached, and cruel. In a way, Hector felt he deserved to be treated this way, since that message had been pounded into him by his father throughout his childhood.

Hector felt worthless, and his lover reinforced this concept through repeated emotional, sexual, and physical abuse. As the situation became unbearable, Hector thought he would die. Thoughts of death pervaded his mind each moment of the day.

Hector finally left this relationship, and over the next few years lived with several other men. He then moved in with a kind, caring young man. Initially, he believed this must be the love he had looked for his entire life. Yet deep in his heart, Hector carried unbearable pain. He still felt incomplete, worthless, disconnected, and alone.

One day, as Hector was walking down the sidewalk, a marquee outside a church caught his eye. The sign announced that a speaker would be discussing the subject of depression that night. All were invited to attend. Hector decided to go.

The speaker told about his life of depression and homosexuality. When he confessed that he had been molested by his grandfather from age three until eleven, Hector had flashbacks of incest involving his own father. Until that moment, he had retained no memory of the abuse. Right there in the meeting, Hector started to weep uncontrollably. He immediately sought help.

After two years of therapy, Hector learned to understand how the abusive experiences of his childhood formed the basis of his depression and the cause of his perpetration of abuse. As he looked back over his life, Hector realized that the years of adult homosexual relationships constituted a vain attempt to regain the love, power, and control missing from his life in order to fill the void left by his abusive, unloving father.

Several of my female clients have told similar stories of being involved in lesbian relationships. Some have been molested or raped by males so they no longer trust men. Others were abused by older females, so their concept of love and sex became distorted. Many had cold, distant mothers. The love they received from their lesbian relationships symbolized the nurturing they never received from their own mothers.

HELP IS AVAILABLE

Whatever self-destructive behaviors you may be struggling with, I urge you to seek help as early as possible. The longer you wait, the more damage will be done, to yourself and to those around you—the people you love and who love you. The sooner you seek help, the sooner your healing process can begin.

Many resources are available for people who struggle with various addictions.

AddictionSolutions.com is an online community for addiction help, education, and resources. They address problems with drugs, alcohol, sex/love, the Internet, gambling, eating disorders, codependency, and nicotine. Their online Treatment Locator can direct you to hotline/helplines, therapist/counseling services, and treatment centers near you.

The Intervention Center, with offices in Washington, DC, and Kensington, Maryland, can be contacted at (301) 588-4558 or toll free at 1-800-422-3213. Their e-mail address is HOWLAND@intervention.com. Their Web site, www.intervention.com, offers resources for alcoholism, drug addiction, gambling, computer addiction, and other compulsive behaviors.

The Illinois Institute for Addiction Recovery offers assistance programs and information for addictions and compulsive behaviors including chemical dependency, gambling, Internet, and sex addiction. The IIAR also offers comprehensive help for addictions in the workplace, food addiction, and compulsive spending. They are located at 5409 N. Knoxville Avenue, Peoria, IL 61614. Phone: (309) 691-1055. Toll free: 1-800-522-3784. Send e-mail to Eric Zehr at zehr@bitwisesystems.com. Web site: www.addictionrecov.org/about.htm.

Alcoholism and Drug Abuse

For those struggling with an addiction to alcohol, Alcoholics Anonymous is an established organization with a tremendous success rate. AA chapters exist all over the world. The General Service Office for the United States and Canada is located at 475 Riverside Drive, New York, NY 10015. Phone: (212) 870-3400. Fax: (212) 870-3003. Their Web site address is www.alcoholics-anonymous.org.

The World Office of the National Institute of Drug Abuse can be reached at P.O. Box 9999, Van Nuys, CA 91409-9999. Phone: (818) 773-9999. Toll-free hotline: 1-800-662-HELP.

The National Council on Alcoholism and Drug Dependence is located at 20 Exchange Place, Suite 2902, New York, NY 10005. Phone: (212) 269-7797. Fax: (212) 269-7510. E-mail: national@ncadd.org. Web site: www.ncadd.org. Twenty-four-hour Hope Line: 1-800-NCA-CALL.

Internet Addiction

The Center for On-Line Addiction offers a variety of resources on "the Psychology of Cyberspace," including a Virtual Clinic that provides direct and affordable telephone or online counseling from the privacy and comfort of your home, office, or school. Their Web site can be found at www.netaddiction.com.

Problem Gambling

Help for obsessive gamblers can be obtained at Gamblers Anonymous. Their International Service Office address is:

P.O. Box 17173, Los Angeles, CA 90017.
Phone: (213) 386-8789. Fax: (213) 386-0030.
E-mail: isomain@gamblersanonymous.org.
Web site: www.gamblersanonymous.org.

Another helpful organization is The Compulsive Gambling Center, Inc:

924 E. Baltimore Street, Baltimore, MD 21202.
Phone: (410) 332-1111. Fax: (410) 685-2307.
Web site: www.compulsivegambctr.com.

The Center has operated a toll-free national hotline since 1987. The current hotline number is 1-800-LOST-BET.

The National Council on Problem Gambling also has a twenty-four-hour confidential, national helpline: 1-800-522-4700.

Sex Addiction

Heart-to-Heart Counseling Centers offers sex addiction recovery resources. Their address is:

P.O. Box 51055, Colorado Springs, CO 80949.
Phone: (719) 278-3708.
E-mail: Heart2Heart@XC.Org.
Web site: www.sexaddict.com.

The "links" page on their Web site includes twelve additional sites, an e-mail forum, and a chat room.

A list of over fifty ministries for homosexuals can be found at:

www.messiah.edu/hpages/
facstaff/chase/h/websites.htm.

One of the largest and most well known is Exodus International. Their mailing address is:

P.O. Box 77652, Seattle, WA 98177.
Phone: (206) 784-7799.
Toll-free in USA: 1-888-264-0877.

CitizenLink, a Web site hosted by Focus on the Family, lists several useful resources for homosexuals at:

www.family.org/cforum/research/papers/a0006891.html. The address for Focus on the Family is 8605 Explorer Drive, Colorado Springs, CO 80995.

THE SYMPTOM OF ABUSE

*O*ne of the most common symptoms of people who have experienced abuse in childhood or adolescence is the presence of various types of abuse in their adult lives.

ABUSE BEGETS FURTHER ABUSE

One common clue that a person has been abused as a child is that she becomes involved in domestic violence and/or sexual abuse as an adult. She may be the victim in a destructive relationship, or she may become an abuser herself.

When the Abuse Continues

When children grow up in homes filled with violence, this becomes their "norm." They assume this is how life is to be lived. Adults who lived in dysfunctional, violent homes have a greater tendency to produce the same type of setting in which to live and raise their children.

Even though the victim doesn't like the abuse, she has learned to survive it. She doesn't know how to behave outside the type of environment she became accustomed to as she was growing up. So she instinctively selects partners who will recreate the familiar scenarios of abuse.

Choosing significant others who are violent gives the victim a warped sense of control because she can re-establish a similar setting to the one she was raised in. This familiarity provides a false sense of security. She knows how to survive in this well-known environment. There are few surprises—abuse and violence have become "normal."

In her distorted view of life, she has no purpose or opportunity to prove she is worthy of love except in meeting the needs of her abuser. She actually feels fortunate to have her abuser, even though he continues to harm her, because he gives her a sense of accomplishment as she meets his selfish demands. She holds on to the false belief that if she can be "good enough," he will love her. However, the perpetrator is incapable of moving beyond his own self-centered desires to appropriately love someone else.

Wanda was raised in what appeared to be an ideal family. Her mother worked at a day-care center and her father was a police officer. She had an older brother and a younger sister. During the day her father protected the citizens of his jurisdiction, but when he came home at night his family became the victims of his violence and abuse.

In counseling with me, Wanda gave accounts of living in terror as her father shouted profanities and threatened her mother if the children were noisy and disrupted his sleep or his television viewing. Frequently she would awaken during the night hearing her mother plead for him to stop his torture and rape.

Wanda's father received several awards for implementing programs to protect women and children, but Wanda and her mother and siblings were constantly criticized and rejected by him. The only time he was involved in their lives was when they participated in community activities. At home he isolated himself behind a locked door that gave him privacy and access to the Internet, where he viewed pornography involving women and children. Hidden in the attic and garage were stacks of pornographic videos and magazines.

After graduating from high school, Wanda moved out of her parents' home and enrolled in a university 300 miles from home. Once she was away from her parents, Wanda became eager to enter the dating scene. Unfortunately, she ended up choosing men who were similar to her father. She took on the role her mother had modeled in the home: powerless, subservient, and valueless. She attempted to gain love and significance from others through unhealthy relationships. This only brought her further pain and rejection.

During her four years of college, Wanda was repeatedly abused mentally, emotionally, physically, and sexually by the men she dated. Upon graduation she accepted a teaching job. To those around her, she appeared happy, confident, and self-assured.

Wanda started dating a young man named Victor, who was highly respected because of his physical attractiveness and outstanding record as a football coach. Shortly after their courtship began, Victor became controlling and abusive.

When a friend noticed bruises on her arms, Wanda denied that the marks had been inflicted by her boyfriend. After persistent questioning, Wanda hesitantly confessed that violence was frequently involved in the times she spent with Victor. But she refused to seek help because she feared a breakup with him.

Since Wanda was raised in an environment of secrecy and violence, she accepted her relationship with Victor as normal. Like her mother, Wanda constantly sought to gain approval and love from her boyfriend through denying her needs in order to meet his.

All through childhood Wanda suffered confusion and a deep sense of worthlessness because of her father's behaviors. She learned to deny her feelings of rejection, abandonment, loneliness, and pain, but underneath this facade was an injured, hurting person whose soul was waging a war against the damaging results of her childhood experiences. The cycle of unmet emotional needs continued.

After much prodding from her friend, Wanda called me for an appointment and began intensive therapy. Her attempt to establish a positive self-esteem has been a long and difficult process. After considerable time, substantial progress was made and she was able to have meaningful relationships for the first time in her life.

When the Abused Becomes the Abuser

As a response to their sense of powerlessness and worthlessness, some adults who were abused in childhood attempt to gain power and release built-up anger by abusing their children, spouses, and others. This self-destructive behavior keeps them "safe," as it reinforces the false belief that they are unworthy of love from others. They actively prevent themselves from entering into meaningful relationships because they don't believe they deserve happiness or fulfillment. To avoid taking responsibility for fostering healthy relationships, they may either withdraw or create chaos to push other people away.

When you don't feel you deserve to be loved, you subconsciously do everything you can to make those who love you take away their love. Your fear of losing love is so intense, you withdraw emotionally and physically to avoid the pain of being rejected. Becoming isolated and detached creates a false sense of safety and allows you freedom from the guilt associated with "undeserved" love.

Venting anger on others can give you a false sense of control over your life. It keeps others from entering your personal world, thus allowing you to avoid the need to trust. Anger and rage become the driving forces in your everyday life.

Alexandra, an obese forty-eight-year-old woman with long stringy hair and dark circles under her eyes, arrived at my office without an appointment at the end of an emotionally draining twelve-hour workday. As I was walking to my car, she approached me, her face contorted with pain. Tears filled her dull, hollow eyes.

"You don't know me," she said. "Nobody does because I'm new in town, but I have to talk to you. I've driven by your office every day for a week, but never had the courage to stop. Tonight I knew if I didn't, I would end up killing myself before morning."

She pulled her tattered sweater more tightly around her. "I can't carry this secret any longer," she continued, "and I can't live with the guilt and shame of it. Will you please help me?"

My initial reaction when I saw her had been to tell her how tired I was and how much I longed to go home. I wanted to explain that my policy was for people to set up an appointment for an evaluation session. But I heard in this woman's voice a desperate cry for help. I knew I couldn't turn her away.

Once we were inside my office, Alexandra began to sob. "My life has always been a disaster," she began. Alexandra was an only child, raised by parents who spent more of their time building a name for themselves in the community and business world than being involved in their daughter's life. Because they traveled a great deal, she was often left with her parents' best friends, who had no children of their own.

During her early teen years, Alexandra began to rebel. At sixteen, she became pregnant. Her parents responded with a consuming concern about how her poor choices would mar their images as Christians, professionals, and parents.

In a desperate attempt to cure Alexandra of her rebellious-ness, her parents took her to see their pastor. He extended a warm embrace to Alexandra's parents. Alexandra herself was briefly acknowledged in an exchange of cold words. She knew the meeting would center more on her parents' needs than hers.

As she sat there, she cried out to herself, *Nobody understands my pain. No one cares about me.* She asked God for the courage to share the deep secret she had carried her entire life.

Knowing she was about to take an enormous risk, Alexandra interrupted the conversation between her parents and their pastor and began telling them about her life of abuse.

"As far back as I can remember," she told her mom and dad, "our neighbors, Mr. and Mrs. Hogren—the ones you left me with all the time—abused me sexually, physically, men-tally, and emotionally."

"What are you talking about?" the pastor asked, stunned.

Alexandra turned away, unable to face him or her parents. "It started when we moved next door to them. I have vague memories from as early as five years old of being fondled by both Mr. and Mrs. Hogren when they babysat me or took me on walks. As I got older the abuse became more intense."

With the floodgates finally open, Alexandra poured out her heart. "Whenever you went out of town and left me with them, the Hogrens undressed me and took my clothes away so I was completely nude the entire time I stayed there. Sometimes other children came, and their clothes were taken from them too. Mr. and Mrs. Hogren made us fondle each other while they watched and gave instructions."

Alexandra told of times when four to six other adults would come to the Hogrens's home, and she was forced to participate in sexual activities with them. Sometimes objects around the house were inserted into her rectum and vagina. Other times the adults used items they had purchased at a porn shop. They were very careful to avoid making marks that would be noticed by anyone.

"I begged you not to make me stay with the Hogrens anymore," Alexandra reminded her parents. "I tried to tell you about the abuse, but you never believed me. Couldn't you tell I was miserable?"

"We did notice that your behavior changed drastically during that time," her mother confessed. "We figured you were simply being rebellious and spoiled."

Alexandra took a deep breath and continued telling her story.

As a young girl, Alexandra often cried at bedtime. She fought to stay awake all night because she dreaded the recurring nightmares. When she awoke crying or screaming, she would get out of bed and try to sleep on the couch or on the floor in her parents' room. Each time her parents caught her, they spanked her and put her back in her bed. She tried telling them about the nightmares filled with monsters, spiders, and animals that were trying to hurt her, but her parents attributed her fears to watching too many scary cartoons and movies.

As she grew up, Alexandra started lying and stealing. She also became infatuated with fire.

One night at age eleven, Alexandra threatened the Hogrens, saying she was going to reveal everything to her parents. The abuse stopped immediately. The Hogrens told Alexandra's parents they could no longer take care of the neighborhood children because they would be taking jobs outside the home. They told Alexandra they would never harm her again as long as she didn't tell her parents. She agreed to keep their secret.

Alexandra still felt enraged, suicidal, and filled with shame. To compensate, she tried to be perfect. Her parents accredited her good behavior and academic achievements to their superior parenting skills.

After years of feeling wretched, Alexandra attempted to regain control of her life. At age fifteen she started sneaking out of the house to meet older boys and men. Although she hated the sexual assaults she suffered at their hands, Alexandra felt validated. She had never been needed by her busy parents or anyone else. These young men at least needed her for sex. They also spent time with her—something her parents rarely did.

Through her promiscuity, Alexandra finally felt she could make decisions about her life. She chose whom she would have sex with, when, and where. In an attempt to gain some control and power in her life, she recreated sexual scenarios similar to the ones she had experienced as a child.

Much to her disappointment, Alexandra found these moments of exhilaration short lived and filled with more guilt, shame, and powerlessness. She told herself she simply had not found the right person and continued to seek out other sexual partners. This began a vicious cycle of sexual experiences that finally resulted in pregnancy.

After Alexandra had divulged the horrors of her childhood, the pastor tapped his fingers and furrowed his brow.

"I've heard a lot of stories in my life from kids who were trying to get themselves out of trouble for their bad decisions," he said, "but this one tops them all. You must have spent an unbelievable amount of time coming up with this story. Too bad you didn't take the time to think about what you were doing instead. Look at what you've done to your parents. I recommend you get your life squared away with

God and learn to take responsibility for your mistakes, young lady." Alexandra's parents agreed wholeheartedly. She felt abandoned and rejected by everyone, including God.

The pastor recommended that she learn how to be responsible for her child, who was going to be born in six months, by doing volunteer work in the church. This, he stated, would be an appropriate punishment for her and would lead her to a godly life.

Realizing that she was powerless to retaliate against her parents and their pastor, Alexandra accepted the assignment. But her anger grew and she began resenting the church and everything it stood for.

Adults had always been abusive and controlling toward her; now it was her turn to determine someone's fate. After Alexandra's son was born, she began to fondle and molest him.

When her son became a teenager, he got a girl pregnant and married her when he was sixteen. He moved to another town, and Alexandra had very little contact with him over the ensuing years.

That night in my office, she cried out to me, "What can you do to change my life?"

"I can't do anything to change your life," I responded gently. "But I know Someone who can." I sensed her anger toward God, but I knew He was her only hope.

"Alexandra," I said, "I can't personally relate to your pain, but I have counseled many people who have had experiences similar to yours. I know you must feel disappointed with God, but He does care for you. He desires to heal you and set you free from your life of suffering and pain."

Dabbing her eyes with tear-soaked tissues, she said, "After all I've done, I deserve nothing but hell."

"You're right," I said, surprising her. "We all deserve the ravages of hell. However, thanks to God's mercy, grace, and love, and because of His Son's shed blood on the cross, we can walk in freedom, redeemed and made new."

Her tears began to dry and she looked up at me with soft eyes. "I don't know why, but for some reason I feel I can trust you. I've never been able to trust anyone. Up to this time, all I've ever heard was that I was a disappointment and a disgrace. I want to hear more about Jesus."

That night, I had the honor of leading Alexandra in the sinner's prayer. What transpired over the next eighteen months was nothing less than miraculous. Through her new relationship with the Lord and intense therapy, God brought about tremendous healing in her life and in her broken family relationships. She sought forgiveness from her son, and they entered into counseling together to work through the issues of abuse and to strengthen their relationship.

Although Alexandra has been forgiven by God, both she and her son will live with the consequences of her actions forever. Being abused never gives a person the right to abuse others. Seeking help as early as possible is absolutely imperative.

Alexandra will never forget her years of being both a victim and a perpetrator, and she deeply regrets the emotional trauma she passed on to her son as a result of the abuse she received. But this repentant woman has been given the gift of grace and love that God desires to give everyone. The first step in obtaining this free gift is making a deliberate choice to accept it. Feelings of forgiveness, love, and acceptance will follow that important decision as you take responsibility for the things you can affect and change, and trust God for the things you can't.

Molesters

Child molesters come from all walks of life. They can be male or female. They may have prestigious careers and social standing. They look no different from those around them. Oftentimes, they attend church and are involved in organizations that promote and protect children. They appear to be loving parents, spouses, and friends.

There are over 300,000 registered sex offenders in the United States today. Sixty percent of them commit new crimes even while under community supervision.[49] The average serial child molester abuses 360 to 380 victims in his lifetime.[50]

THE IMPACT OF SEXUAL ABUSE ON CHILDREN

According to the U.S. Department of Justice, the percentage by age of victims of sexual assault reported to law enforcement agencies breaks down as follows.[51]

- 67 percent were juveniles (under the age of eighteen).
- 34 percent were under age twelve.
- One out of every seven victims was under age six.

Children Assaulting Children

Frequently, the person who sexually molests a child is also a child. ChildHelp USA® reports that 40 percent of the

---

49 Texas Sex Offenders Registry Web site: http://sexoffenderregistry.net/texas/texas-sex-offenders.htm.

50 "South Carolina Other Forcible Sex Crimes, Summary," South Carolina Law Enforcement Division, Columbia, SC, 1999.

51 "Sexual Assault of Young Children as Reported to Law Enforcement: Victim, Incident, and Offender Characteristics," U.S. Department of Justice, Bureau of Justice Statistics, 7/00 NCJ 182990. (See Web site: http://www.ojp.usdoj.gov/bjs/abstract/saycrle.htm.)

offenders who sexually assaulted children under age six were juveniles (under eighteen).[52]

In their powerless state, abused children turn their anger on younger victims. This is an attempt to regain what was taken from them—personal power and control—and to express their disapproval of what has taken place. It is imperative that abused children are given the help they need as quickly as possible. The sooner a child begins therapy, the less likely he will become an abuser.

Nobody Understands the Children's Pain

I love working with children. But I become deeply frustrated when the cries for help from severely traumatized kids are not heard or understood by the adults around them.

Because they are young, their verbal skills are limited. Their accounts of abuse are often invalidated by their perpetrators and authorities because they lack the emotional strength, memory skills, and appropriate words to give an accurate description of the abuse they endured.

Sometimes children are unable to provide details of the abuse they have suffered because the memories are so traumatic.

Children are often fearful of the consequences of disclosure. A child may still love her abuser and want to spend time with him. Young children often equate abusive sexual experiences with love, believing those acts are indications that they are "special" to the perpetrator. Oftentimes, they do not understand that what happened to them was wrong.

---

[52] "Sexual Assault of Young Children as Reported to Law Enforcement: Victim, Incident, and Offender Characteristics," July 2000, NCJ 182990. (Findings from the National Incident-Based Reporting System. Data based on reports from law enforcement agencies for years 1991 through 1996. See U.S. Department of Justice Bureau of Justice Statistics Web site, www.ojp.usdoj.gov/bjs.)

All they know is that part of the experience made them feel good. They liked the closeness and attention. In order to cope with the unwanted feelings, many of the details of the trauma are pushed into the crevices of their subconscious, allowing the child to escape, at least temporarily, their horrible and tormenting experience. They may not want to disclose what they do remember for fear that they will lose contact with the parent they feel so close to.

Honesty does not necessarily increase with age. Young children are basically honest, taking on dishonest traits as they emulate adults around them. So if a child claims to have been abused, chances are good that she is telling the truth. Children are not born with an inherent ability to describe demeaning sexual acts. They can only give detailed reports of such experiences if they have personally lived them.

Even young people who have not been abused have difficulty remembering details of past events. But recent medical research has revealed profound discoveries on the correlation between abuse and the function of the brain. The October 1995 issue of *Scientific American*[53] reported that many men and women who have been subjected to severe physical or sexual abuse during childhood suffer from long-term disturbances of the psyche. They may experience nightmares and flashbacks—much like survivors of war—or they may become extremely calm, almost numb, in situations of extreme stress.

That same article cited two recent studies that indicated survivors of child abuse may have a smaller hippocampus (the part of the brain that forms, stores, and processes memory) than people who have not been abused. Changes in the

---

[53] Madhusree Mukerjee, "Hidden Scars: Sexual and other abuse may alter a brain region," *Scientific American*, NY, (237:4) 10/95.

hippocampus could be brought about by hormones flooding the brain during and after a stressful episode.

This explains one reason abused children and adults tend to have trouble building healthy relationships and self-esteem. It may also help us understand why abused children have such a difficult time with behavior and learning.

When she becomes inundated with emotions she can't control or explain, an abused child may begin to lie, steal, or play with fire. These cries for help exemplify the secrecy, power, and control the child experienced in her personal trauma. She is hoping someone will notice her behavior, ask the right questions, and come to her rescue.

Unfortunately, during a typical investigation or in a court of law, these negative behaviors can be used against the young victim. The child is portrayed as a "bad" person who can't be believed or trusted.

The child's account of the abuse may vary somewhat from reality. As his mind seeks to protect him from the distressing memories, trivial details such as the color of clothing the perpetrator was wearing seem insignificant and so may not be recalled accurately. Such details should not be considered when investigating child abuse. Behaviors, signs, and symptoms exhibited by the child must be taken into more serious consideration. Unfortunately, investigators tend to latch onto discrepancies in a child's story and inter-pret them to mean that the child is being untruthful.

At this point a child may become overwhelmed and inca-pable of handling his emotions. He fears the punishment and consequences of not being believed. He worries about rejection. He feels alienated and alone. Sensing that everyone has aban-doned him, he says he "just made the story up." At that point, carrying his secret pain appears much easier than trying to cope with a new problem—proving his innocence.

When this happens the legal accusations against the abuser are shattered and the case is dropped. The perpetrator escapes sentencing and the child becomes victimized by "the system."

As the public gains a better understanding of the signs, symptoms, and effects of abuse, more perpetrators will be given the verdicts they deserve. Prosecution for this crime will be more successful when children's accounts of abuse are given more serious consideration and their behaviors better understood.

I grieve deeply every time a perpetrator of child abuse succeeds in discounting the testimony of an abused child. When this happens, the child's right to a life of innocence and safety is stolen by the abuser. The deception allows abusers to continue destroying other children through mental, emotional, physical, or sexual abuse.

Concerned citizens and child advocates must work together to promote changes in the law that will enforce stiffer penalties for sexual offenses committed against children and adults. When abusers are given probation for first-time offenses, every person in society is placed at risk of being abused. "First-time offenses" are often simply the first time the abuser's crime was reported. If placed on probation, the perpetrator should be required to attend offender classes and counseling.

Katie was a beautiful eleven-year-old girl who was molested at the age of seven by her aunt. This woman had a long history of lying and criminal violations, including writing bad checks and using illegal drugs. At the time Katie reported the abuse, her aunt was serving time in a Washington state prison and was scheduled to be up for probation within a few months.

Katie's family feared the abusive aunt would retaliate by harming the child for disclosing the abuse. In an effort to keep her safe, they moved to Texas.

Later, when Katie was brought into a courtroom to testify, she became terrified as she sat across from her abusive aunt. Fear overtook her and she was suddenly unable to recount various details of the abuse. During the court proceedings, her aunt told the authorities and jurors that Katie's story had been fabricated either by the child or by her parents. The case was dismissed and the aunt walked away without any consequences for her heinous crime.

What might a child's interpretation of a court's decision like this be?

- We don't listen to children.
- We don't believe you.
- You have no value or worth.
- It's okay for adults to abuse you.
- Children should be seen and not heard.
- You have no rights—not even the right to stop being abused.
- You have no pain.

With the dismissal of this case and the invalidation she received, Katie has a high potential for further abuse, addictions, and a life filled with anger and revenge. I have worked with numerous clients who have committed such crimes as arson, stealing, and using illegal drugs and alcohol, and in most cases, these clients were abused early in life. They were seeking comfort and relief from their past, desperately searching for power and control. *Nobody understood their pain.*

Recent Statistics of Child Abuse

In September 2003, ChildHelp USA® compiled these startling statistics.[54]

- More than 2.67 million reports of possible maltreatment involving 3 million children were made to child protective service agencies in 2001.[55] The actual incidence of abuse and neglect is estimated to be three times greater than the number reported to authorities.[56]

- In 2001, an estimated 1,300 children died of abuse and neglect—an average of more than three children per day. Of these fatalities, 84.5 percent were under the age of six; 41 percent of the children were under the age of one.[57]

---

[54] Based on April 2003 reports of the U.S. Department of Health and Human Services, Administration for Children and Families (www.acf.hhs.gov).

[55] U.S. Department of Health and Human Services, Administration on Children, Youth and Families, Child Maltreatment 2001 (Washington, DC: US Government Printing Office, 2003). (See Web site: www.acf.hhs.gov/programs/cb/publications/cm01/outcover.htm.)

[56] U.S. Department of Health and Human Services, National Center on Child Abuse and Neglect. Third National Incidence Study of Child Abuse and Neglect: Final Report (NIS-3), Washington, D.C.: Government Printing Office, September 1996.

[57] U.S. Department of Health and Human Services, Administration on Children, Youth and Families, Child Maltreatment 2001 (Washington, DC: US Government Printing Office, 2003). (See Web site: www.acf.hhs.gov/programs/cb/publications/cm01/outcover.htm.)

- More children (age four and younger) die from child abuse and neglect than from falls, choking on food, suffocation, drowning, residential fires, and motor vehicle accidents.[58]

- Homicide is the leading cause of injury deaths among infants in the United States. Perpetrators are typically the mother, father, or stepfather.[59]

Children today are at a greater risk of being abused than ever before. Many factors contribute to this increase, including more stressful home environments, single-parent families, teen parents, lack of financial stability, unresolved issues of abuse, drugs, alcohol, and pornography. These abused children will grow up to become abusive adults, which will raise these already horrific statistics to an even greater level . . . unless these victims receive appropriate counseling to learn how to deal with abuse and stop the cycle.

For additional up-to-date statistics about child abuse, see "In Fact . . . Answers to Frequently Asked Questions on Child Abuse and Neglect," a fact sheet that synthesizes information from several federally supported sources.[60]

---

[58] "A Nation's Shame: Fatal Child Abuse and Neglect in the United States," U.S. Department of Health and Human Services, Advisory Board on Child Abuse and Neglect, April 1995 (based upon figures from the National Safety Council and the Centers for Disease Control and Prevention).

[59] "Infant Homicide," a report issued by Child Trends, an independent research organization, December 2002. (See Web site: www.childtrends-databank.org.)

[60] National Clearinghouse on Child Abuse and Neglect Information, Washington, DC. (See www.eccac.org/other/faqcan.htm.)

BREAKING THE CYCLE

You can begin the process of healing and start living a normal, healthy life once you understand and acknowledge the effects of abuse. First you must restructure your way of thinking, a task that will probably require outside help to accomplish. In the past you have developed coping skills that allowed you to survive the abuse. Now you must acquire new skills to break the cycle of abuse and avoid future abusive relationships.

Decide right now that you will no longer be a victim.

THE REWARDS

Although the recovery process can be frightening, it can be a tremendous opportunity for growth. What begins as a time of intense fear can become your greatest walk of boldness and faith. You can gain strength and courage that will allow you to fulfill your goals and dreams. Through this experience you can come to know Christ in a way you have never understood Him before. You can learn to let go of self-control and let God control your life. You can learn to trust and love yourself and others.

Even though trusting has been difficult in the past, I assure you that God desires good things for your life. The journey is frightening, but healing from your abusive past is worth the effort.

CHAPTER 6

COPING MECHANISMS

*C*oping mechanisms (also called "defense mechanisms") are used to create a sense of stability in the
life of an individual who feels threatened or is in a painful or
stressful situation. While most coping behaviors are learned
through modeling, some are instinctive and appear when
needed.

Both learned and innate behaviors manifest in various
ways to meet the needs of the user. Defense mechanisms can
be good or bad. They are good when they are used short term
to get us through a crisis. They become bad when they are
utilized long term and the person using them avoids working through her issues or problems.

Victims of abuse must initially depend on various
defense methods for their survival. Coping skills allow a
victim temporary relief from her pain. They allow her to
have a sense of control over the feelings associated with her
traumatic experiences.

However, sufferers of abuse must be willing to let go of
unhealthy methods of coping and replace them with healthy
methods in order to heal from the devastating effects of their
abusive experiences.

DENIAL

Many abusers and abuse victims do not realize they are in
a destructive situation. They hide the abuse by denying it

exists. They distort reality by redefining the meaning of abuse. They adjust what they consider to be right and wrong. Ultimately, any act, no matter how hideous, can be carried out with a fairly clear conscience once a person has developed the necessary level of denial.

Denial, at its most basic, means lying to self and to others. You say that something never happened when you know it did. Denial allows you to continue harming other people, or being harmed by those you love, by refusing to accept that the actions are wrong.

Denial can be extremely powerful. If you lie to yourself about something often enough and strongly enough, you may actually come to believe the lie.

The road to serious abuse is usually traveled in several small steps. By committing or putting up with "little" abuses, you bring yourself closer to the state where more dangerous exploitations are committed.

The major tactics used in maintaining denial are *minimizing*, *rationalizing*, and *justifying*.

Minimizing

Minimizing distances you from traumatic experiences by claiming the damage wasn't as bad as it was. For example, "I didn't beat her; I just pushed her."

By minimizing the damage, an abuser can blame the victim for "exaggerating" the abuse. The abuser may even accuse the victim of making the whole thing up.

If the abuse can be proven, the abuser may show partial repentance. "I'll accept the responsibility of anything you can prove, but nothing more."

Rationalizing

Rationalization consists of lying to yourself about what was done in order to make it seem acceptable. "She's lucky I only hit her once. Anybody else would have beaten the daylights out of her." These acceptable-sounding lies are repeated until you can convince yourself of anything . . . particularly when admitting the truth becomes more and more painful.

Justifying

Justification is explaining why something abusive was acceptable. "She drove me to it," for example.

When people are abusing others they are usually incapable of separating themselves from their behavior. Admitting that the behavior is bad would make the perpetrator of that behavior "bad" as well. Nobody wants to think of himself that way.

Often, an abuser will use a combination of all three aspects of denial. "It was okay for me to threaten to kill her (justifying). She was getting so upset I had to shut her up before she disturbed the neighbors (rationalizing). Besides, I didn't really mean it (minimizing). She knows I could never hurt her."

Denial allows abusers to live with what they've done. It can also enable a victim to live with what has been done to her. It keeps them functioning in a situation they would not otherwise survive.

How To Recognize Denial

Denial is so powerful that an abuser can look someone in the eye and tell an outright lie, even believing it himself. So how can you tell if you (or someone you love) are using this destructive coping mechanism?

• "But . . ."

Statements that follow the word *but* are frequently denial. "I know it's wrong to yell at her like that, *but* she really upsets me."

- **"You don't understand . . ."**

The phrase *you don't understand* is also a tip-off. "Usually I'd consider that to be abusive. But *you don't understand* how mad she makes me. She can really push my buttons sometimes."

If someone is in denial, he is usually unwilling to listen to professionals. He rationalizes his actions by saying that the experts "don't know what they're talking about, at least in this instance." The abuser believes that his ideas are more accurate than those of others. This conclusion is based on the concept that his situation is so unique that the rules that apply to others don't apply to him.

- **"At least I'm not . . ."**

Anytime someone compares himself to someone else, he is probably justifying something he knows to be wrong. "Man, that guy really treats his wife like garbage. I never call my wife the names he does. And I never swear when I'm yelling. Boy, he's really out of control. I'm glad I'm not like him. I wonder why she puts up with him." No matter who you are, or how bad your actions are, you can always find someone worse. But that doesn't make what you're doing right.

- **"It's not my fault because . . ."**

Blaming others for what's wrong with you is a form of denial. "I never would have hit her that hard if she hadn't called her ex-boyfriend. I don't know what it's going to take to make her stop. If she'd only listen to me, I wouldn't get so mad at her."

- **"I can't change . . ."**

Virtually anything followed by "That's just the way I am" is denial.

If you remain in doubt as to whether or not something is denial, ask someone who does not have an interest in maintaining the facade. Don't ask your drug dealer if you have a drug problem; ask a counselor. If you are afraid to do this, you are most likely in denial.

Denying that there is a problem, or rationalizing away the reasons, puts family members and other loved ones in danger of escalating violence that could lead to serious injury or even death. Ignoring the painful realities of abuse does not make them go away. It only allows them to grow more painful and ugly.

The Damaging Effects of Denial

Ginny was an attractive young woman who had lived her entire life with alcoholic parents. She was an only child and felt responsible for making her family look good in the community. Ginny excelled in academics and sports. She attended church on a regular basis and was respected by both peers and adults. But Ginny felt ambivalent toward her parents because of their lack of support. She had little trust or respect for either of them.

For years, Ginny made excuses for her parents' lack of involvement in her life. She also denied that her father's inappropriate touches and comments were sexual in nature. She rationalized that this was his way of showing he loved her. Besides, he had "shown her his love" in this manner for as long as she could remember. She regarded his constant viewing of pornographic Web sites and magazines as "something all men do."

Ginny dated very little in high school and college. As she grew older, her distrust in men became stronger.

When she entered the business world, her job involved extensive travel and meetings with men. She dated occasionally, but refused to make a commitment until she met Harry, a handsome young businessman who came from a family where both parents were alcoholics. Ginny trusted him because they had much in common. She felt he *understood her pain*. For the first time, she was able to face her fears and begin the process of learning to trust another human being.

Harry was involved with several women when he met Ginny, but he vowed to be faithful to her if she would commit to a long-term relationship with him. After a nine-month courtship and a three-month engagement, they were married. Ginny and Harry were excited to have finally found the monogamous relationship they had always dreamed of— filled with love, trust, honesty, and respect.

Six months into the marriage, however, Ginny began to have concerns about Harry's faithfulness. He had been coming home late on a regular basis. After she went to sleep at night, he would get out of bed and view pornography and talk to women in a chat room on the Internet.

One day Ginny found a pair of eyeglasses in his car. When she confronted Harry, he dismissed her concerns and claimed that he had been working on a special project with a female employee and had given her a ride home. He assured her the glasses must have accidentally fallen out of her purse and that he had never been alone with her other than at work.

Ginny feared her marriage was in a major crisis. She was two months pregnant with their first baby, and the thought of raising the child alone was more than she could bear. She chose to handle this situation as she had done with unpleasant circumstances in her childhood: deny her feelings and pretend her life was normal.

Ginny minimized the effects of Harry's behavior by telling herself that if she wasn't pregnant, she wouldn't feel as worried about his relationships with other women.

She justified that if she hadn't gained weight during the pregnancy, he would find her more attractive and wouldn't need other women. Since she felt physically unappealing, Ginny struggled to be the perfect wife in an attempt to gain Harry's affirmation and respect.

After the birth of their child, Harry continued his abusive lifestyle. Three years later he was arrested at his office late one night for soliciting a prostitute who was an undercover agent. Ginny came to his defense, taking responsibility for his behavior and stating that after their child was born, she had stopped meeting his sexual needs satisfactorily.

Harry was never prosecuted. Eight months later, Ginny received a phone call from a friend who reported that she had seen Harry coming out of a motel with another woman in a small community forty-five miles away from where they lived.

Finally, Ginny decided she could no longer live with Harry's unfaithfulness. They both came in for counseling. Harry eventually realized that his sexual addiction did not begin as an adult but as a six-year-old child who was introduced to pornography by teenage boys in his neighborhood. Harry remembered the overwhelming sense of shock, fear, and disbelief he experienced the first time he was shown pictures of nude women in magazines. From that moment on, he had little respect for women and saw them only as sex objects.

Harry's early exposure to pornography made him intrigued with sex, which left him vulnerable to sexual abuse. He spent the next seven years of his life attempting to survive the ravages of sexual assault from ruthless men who preyed upon him in the absence of his alcoholic father.

As Harry finally associated his adult behaviors with his issues of abuse, addiction, and abandonment, Ginny discovered she had used the same coping skills in her marriage that she had used to survive living with alcoholic parents. Together they committed to begin the long, difficult road to wholeness.

The Cure for Denial

The only cure for denial is to give up the charade and admit the reality. The longer you stay in denial, the longer you delay your healing.

No one can force someone to face the truth. However, the use of honesty and accountability can go a long way toward helping someone move from denial to recovery.

OTHER COPING MECHANISMS

Denial is the most common method for coping with abuse in one's past, but it is not the only one. Following are descriptions of other ways people attempt to cope with tragic life circumstances.

Dissociation

Dissociation is commonly seen in people who have been abused. It allows you some measure of control over your haunting memories by removing them from your conscious memory. Eventually it becomes an automatic response toward any person or activity that threatens your physical or emotional well-being.

Dissociating whenever you experience uncomfortable feelings allows you to discount or minimize the abuse as being insignificant and having no effect on your life. People who dissociate often say, "I was abused as a child, but it didn't really affect me." Yet they are filled with anger, fear, and powerlessness.

This defense mechanism allows you to cope, but it prevents you from recovering from the traumatic incident.

The expression "What you don't feel will never heal" applies here. If you do not acknowledge your pain, you will never heal from its scathing effects.

Children who cannot escape from the threat of abuse often mentally withdraw from a horrific situation by separating themselves from conscious awareness of their circumstances. They may create a "safe place" by regressing to an earlier stage in life, a time before the abuse occurred. They "stand still" emotionally and do not progress beyond the time of the abuse. This coping mechanism enables the victim to detached herself from the situation, as if what is happening is not really happening to her. This emotional shut-down will follow them throughout their lifetime unless they seek help.

Many psychiatrists believe that if dissociation is repeatedly invoked in childhood, it will prevent memories from being integrated into consciousness and can lead to an altered sense of self.

Creating New Personalities

On rare occasions, people actually develop a true Multiple Personality Disorder, which is a complex, chronic form of post-traumatic dissociative psychopathology. However, anyone who has experienced abuse may selectively create new personalities in her mind as a means of escape.

Children who use this coping device have extraordinary imaginations. When a child who has been abused encounters overpowering emotions, he may choose to escape into a safer personality, one who hasn't been abused, in order to detach himself from the memories and pain.

Many normal children play with imaginary companions; abused children can use such creative resources to a pathological extent, in extreme cases falling prey to MPD.

Robert was a nine-year-old boy who lived with his parents and a three-year-old brother, Billy. Robert was brought in for counseling because his mother witnessed him performing digital penetration on Billy when they were bathing together. The mother once found her sons in a bedroom closet with Robert fondling Billy. Robert had become overly inquisitive about his mother's private body parts and would attempt to touch her inappropriately if he walked in on her while she was bathing or changing clothes.

Robert began sucking his thumb and soiling his underwear, something he had not done since he was three years old. He had not been sleeping well at night due to repeated nightmares of spiders, snakes, animals, monsters, and people chasing him. His mother and father discounted the nightmares as the result of hearing scary stories from his older cousins and blamed his other problems on a lack of sleep.

Robert's behavior was extremely unpredictable. His parents reported that at times it seemed as if he had two different personalities. He had a vivid imagination and engaged in fantasy quite often. He would pretend to be a hero figure who conquered evil people and wild animals.

Robert started displaying a great deal of aggression at home and at school—always hitting his siblings and defying his teacher and school rules. He would go for periods of time when his behavior returned to normal, then without apparent reason, he would erupt into rages and be out of control again. His grades plummeted. He was sad and moody and would isolate himself in his room. He refused to go back to the lake or to the community swimming pool, which he used to love to visit.

One day Robert's parents were called in to the school for a conference. The teacher and the principal informed the parents that Robert would be taken out of the regular classroom until his behavior improved and he was no longer a threat to the other children. At that point, his mother called me for an appointment.

Progress in therapy was slow until Robert's third session, when I informed him that I was preparing a speech to present to adults about helping children who experienced bad things. I asked him if he could help me out by teaching me what he knew about little boys and girls who had bad things happen to them. I asked him if he knew of anyone like that.

Robert immediately told me the story of a little boy name Joey who had gone to the lake with his parents for a family reunion. Joey went swimming near where his family was visiting with relatives. His older cousin was told to keep an eye on him, but she was distracted by her friends, who were also at the lake.

As Robert continued telling Joey's story, he began to tremble and suck his thumb. He reported that when Joey was playing in the lake, he met a man who told him he would take him out in the deep water and teach him some fun tricks. Joey said he didn't want to go into the deep water, but the man took hold of him and forced him to go far away from shore.

Tears filled Robert's eyes as his trembling and thumb-sucking intensified. "Joey was really scared," he said. "He thought he was going to die and never see his family again."

When I asked Robert what happened next, he gave graphic accounts of Joey being molested.

With fear in his eyes, Robert added, "The man said that if Joey ever told anybody what happened, he would find him and his little brother and drown both of them. Then he told Joey to stay in the water until he got in his car and left."

I thanked Robert for his help and praised him for his bravery in relating the story. I then asked, "Robert, is there something else you want to tell me about this?" I reminded him that he was safe and no one would hurt him.

He sat quietly for a few minutes. Finally, he looked up and said, "It was me."

I asked him to clarify what he meant.

"The boy who got bad touches at the lake . . . that was me."

After finishing my interview with Robert, I informed his parents of the disclosure. I described to them the steps I had to take to report the abuse. As they sat there in shock, they began to trace Robert's changes in behavior to the time of the incident at the lake.

Perfectionism

Attempting to be perfect frequently becomes the prevailing life goal of a victim of abuse. Because she has such a low opinion of herself, the victim assumes that others see her as damaged and flawed, incapable of making worthwhile contributions. She is convinced that everyone she comes in contact with can see the scars and flaws in her life. She believes that people see her as incompetent, crazy, dirty, nasty, and bad. Some victims strive to make their outside world look good, hoping this will serve as a shield to blind others from seeing who they really are.

No matter how hard you try to be perfect, you can never achieve this impossible goal. Whatever accomplishments you gain will be perceived by you as accidental or insignificant. You can always find someone who is better than you are and has garnered more victories. Family and friends may see you as successful, but you refuse to believe them, wondering if they are patronizing you, perhaps even lying to you. You become angry because you feel your loved ones are secretly thinking, *Considering the kind of person she is, I guess this is the best she can do.*

If you get tired of trying to be perfect, you may adopt a new attitude: *If I don't try, then I won't fail.* This thought process eventually dominates every area of your life, permeating your relationships, careers, even daily activities. This powerless state of mind makes you an easy target for further damaging experiences.

When perfectionism fails, you may try to cope with your traumatic experiences by becoming *perfectly bad.* By engaging in a series of continually worse behaviors, you attempt to send a message that says, "No one will ever hurt me again. I'll hurt you before you can hurt me."

As a result of never feeling either "good enough" or "bad enough," you keep yourself unapproachable to individuals who may wish to support you. You spend your life lonely, alone, and isolated from the world.

Creating Chaos To Gain Control

When you do not trust yourself or others around you, you start to feel out of control. You may try to regain control by creating chaos in relationships in which you feel safe.

Since you cannot control your own life or behavior, you feel empowered as you push the emotional "buttons" of loved ones and cause their behaviors and lives to change. Several dynamics are taking place that are usually unknown to both the victim and the people drawn into her turmoil.

If you are involved in an abusive relationship, you may "act out" as a means of gaining the attention of people who might ask the right questions about your behavior. This would allow you an opportunity to disclose the violation that is taking place and be rescued from the abuser.

Children and teenagers are especially prone to creating chaos in the "I need to be rescued" phase. They refuse to comply with rules at home or at school. They initiate verbal or physical confrontations with people who are in authority over them, including the legal system. They may strive to engage in conflict with others who make them look bad or with whom they feel inferior. This may include siblings or friends who have never experienced abuse. They become jealous, perceiving that these individuals are more loved or protected by parents and others.

Even if you are no longer involved in an abusive situation, you may create chaos as a reaction to the self-hate, anger, and rage you carry inside you. You hurt deeply, and the only option you see is to inflict pain on others. This action does relieve your anguish, but only temporarily. As the conflicts subside, you quickly devise ways to cause more upheaval in order to regain control.

Common behaviors adults use to create chaos include excessive drinking, use of illegal drugs, promiscuity, stealing, lying, sabotaging relationships, behaving irresponsibly, and even self-mutilation. For most people, physical pain seems easier to deal with and control than emotional pain. By injuring himself, the victim attempts to recreate the pain of the abuse while maintaining control over its execution. Self-injury allows the victim to transfer his pain from the emotional to the physical realm. Taking control over his pain provides him with a false sense of empowerment and temporary relief.

The negative behaviors described above, even self-mutilation, can become addictive and difficult to stop. Each instance reinforces the thought pattern of *I am bad and worthless, deserving to be punished.*

Obsession with Meeting the Needs of Others

Victims of abuse often become consumed with meeting the needs of other people, even at the expense of their own well-being.

Your problems appear so enormous that conquering them seems like an overwhelming, impossible task. Feeling inadequate to control your life, you subconsciously look for someone you can "fix" or "rescue." You take on the responsibility for keeping your loved ones safer than you were able to keep yourself.

A commonly used term for this behavior is *codependence*. You become involved in a codependent relationship with another traumatized person because you see traits and deficiencies of yourself in that person. Since you couldn't save yourself, you feel it is your responsibility to free your codependent partner from the destructive relationships in his life. Your unconscious goal is to empower yourself, but this effort becomes blurred by the flurry of activities and emotional energies spent trying to meet the other person's needs.

Characteristics of codependency include caretaking (both emotionally and physically), lack of validation, controlling behaviors, dependency, weak boundaries, enmeshment, lack of trust, anger, and fear.

Detachment

Detachment is a pattern of behavior commonly seen in victims of abuse. It is characterized by general aloofness in relationships. You are unable to become attached to others because doing so in the past resulted in excruciating injuries that still torment you.

To avoid further harm, you live your life in a vacuum. You appear to be unaffected by people or events in daily life. To maintain safety, no one is allowed to enter your private world. The extent of detachment usually correlates to the degree of trust you had in your attacker. If you knew the perpetrator personally, especially if you were related to him, this will intensify your inability to trust.

The detached person acts cold and uncaring toward others. You may appear to have an attitude of entitlement: "I deserve to get everything I want because the world has wronged me." Seeking to meet your basic needs, you solicit help from others to obtain money and material goods.

Yet when you get this help, you lack any show of appreciation for it. Your inability to respond leaves those seeking to help you feeling angry, rejected, hurt, and used. By detaching yourself from your feelings, you become oblivious to the pain you create in the lives of others.

OVERCOMING COPING MECHANISMS

To change these self-destructive behaviors, negative coping mechanisms must be replaced with positive methods of dealing with pain. Until this happens, life is a vicious cycle of chaos and defeat. Both you and your family and friends lose to the monster called *abuse.*

To develop new ways of coping, change must take place. No one can change you. You can't change another person. Change comes from within. People can support and encourage you as you change, but they can't do the work for you.

One of the most powerful ways to bring about change is to transform the way you think about yourself. This can only come about by replacing the self-defeating messages that play in your mind. Replacing cynical thinking patterns with positive, reinforcing thoughts will help change your view of who you are and what you deserve in life.

You must not allow negative, self-defeating talk from within or from others to assault you. If you are still in an abusive relationship, develop a plan that will allow you to be safe, both emotionally and physically. This usually involves locating a new place to live, making arrangements to have your financial needs met, and having a support system in place.

As you gain a better understanding of your right to be respected and valued, you take on a new identity. Old negative ways of coping will be replaced with healthy, constructive ones that allow you the freedom to experience life in a more meaningful and satisfying way.

SEEKING HELP

ictims of abuse have difficulty asking for help. Terrorized by fear and feeling powerless to change your situation, you may survive temporarily by using denial or other coping mechanisms. But after a while, these stopgap measures can no longer control the pain. Eventually, you will be forced to face the reality of your maltreatment. You must then make the decision to either cry out for help or give in to the enemy. If you choose to give in, your spirit will die a slow, agonizing death.

When an abused person finally does cry out for help, it is not because she suddenly becomes empowered and loses her fears, but because she has reached a point of total despair and hopelessness. Emotionally you have already begun the process of dying. You've grown numb to your perpetrator's threats to harm you further if you disclose the abuse. You may even consider death a welcome relief to the unbearable pain.

Unfortunately, sometimes abuse does culminate in a victim's death, or in lifelong injuries that may seem like an even worse fate. But no one has to live in despair forever. Help is available through counseling and the power of prayer.

WHY A VICTIM MAY NOT SEEK HELP
Fear

Because your ability to trust has been damaged by your abuse, you don't feel safe disclosing your secret to anyone.

In addition, your abuser may have threatened to harm you, or someone you love, if you ever tell. You may also be afraid of being judged for your negative behaviors and poor choices rather than receiving the support you need.

If you've been carrying your secret for a long time, seeking help can seem more frightening than remaining quiet. Whenever you consider disclosing the abuse—whether to a friend, family member, or professional counselor—fear-provoking questions plague you:

> *What if people don't believe me?*
> *What if they think it was my fault?*
> *What if they no longer want to be my friends?*
> *What if they don't maintain confidentiality?*
> *What if they start treating me differently?*
> *What if they think I've become an abuser?*
> *What if they see me as dirty, bad, and flawed?*
> *What if my abuser finds out I told?*

These fears can become paralyzing, causing you to stall in your process of healing even at this early stage.

Perhaps you are experiencing one or more of the following fears.

• Greater loss

Sometimes, as horrible as the abuse is, the consequences for seeking help can seem even more devastating. You may fear the loss of your reputation as well as the love and respect of others, who may reject you if they find out what has been happening in your life. You may feel so afraid of the consequences of leaving your abuser that you stay in the demeaning relationship . . . until the assaults become so unbearable you would rather die than continue living with the pain.

• No longer being needed

You might feel afraid of no longer being needed, even if the only need you fulfill is the perpetrator's need to abuse you.

• Lack of belief

You may fear that no one will believe you because you did not report the abuse earlier, or because you stayed in the relationship as long as you did.

• No support

Perhaps you fear that no one will want to support you because you ignored everyone's advice to get out of the relationship sooner. You may fear that everyone will think you got what you deserved.

• Vulnerability

You may struggle with the fear of becoming vulnerable and being abused by others who offer their help.

• Survival

You might wonder how you will survive if you leave your abuser. This course of action is especially frightening if it requires finding your own housing and a way to support yourself.

• Not enough strength

Maybe you are afraid you won't be strong enough to go through the healing process. You may even fear that you are too damaged to heal, that you are forever worthless, hopeless, and marked.

• The unknown

Because you have become accustomed to the abuse, it becomes your norm. You may have never experienced a sound relationship and simply do not know which behaviors are acceptable and which are not.

• Admission

You may be afraid of acknowledging just how badly you were abused.

• No understanding

You probably fear that *nobody will understand your pain.*

Powerlessness

The emotional and/or physical injuries you have suffered may appear too complex and overwhelming to conquer. You desire to walk in freedom, but the ravages of your harmful experiences have become strongholds in your life, leaving you feeling powerless to change your circumstances.

You may not even know why you stay in the destructive relationship. Perhaps you don't understand your own powerlessness. You don't realize you can say no to your abuser. The perpetrator has played mind games and manipulated you into thinking you owe him something for what you receive from the relationship. He convinces you that you are to blame for his abusive behavior, claiming that your shortcomings cause him to act abusively. You are blinded to the fact that he disrespects you and is using you for his own personal gain of power and control.

Unfortunately, no amount of power is ever enough. The never-ending quest for control becomes more challenging, and the victimization becomes more severe, with each new encounter. The perpetrator constantly has to take the abuse to a more extensive level in order to receive personal satisfaction and empowerment.

Any relationship in which personal boundaries are not respected is unhealthy and leaves the victim feeling like damaged goods. No one should be forced to engage in any activity, sexual or otherwise, that is against his will or is not affirming and pleasantly meaningful.

Healthy relationships are not about living in fear, trade-offs, or keeping score. They involve loving, caring, nurturing, respecting, supporting, and sacrificing for each other so each person can reach his or her full potential. In a loving, healthy relationship, each partner desires more for the other person than he wants for himself. Healthy relationships promote mutual growth and individuality.

Bad Advice

Unfortunately, when victims of abuse finally make the choice to disclose their secret, they are often given advice that, rather than helping, can cause even further damage.

• "Just Have Faith"

Many times in the Christian community, the panacea for all that ails an individual is to *"Just have faith!"* Faith is incredibly important and necessary every single moment of our lives, especially when we are going through trying times. Ultimate healing comes through faith in the Great Physician, Jehovah Rapha. But sometimes God leads us to people such as doctors, pastors, counselors, or lay people in order to receive the help we need to go through the process of healing.

Abuse victims who are Christians will struggle further if they are led to believe that they don't need outside help, that their faith should be sufficient to heal them. If this simplistic solution prevents you from seeking the counseling you need, your pain and scars will become more severe and deeply rooted. Your emotional baggage will increase with each failed relationship and poor decision.

Real faith does not deny that abuse has taken place. Nor does it claim that abuse has not had a major impact on you. Having faith does not mean you simply repress or push aside the traumatic experience and go on as if it never occurred. On the contrary, faith allows you to face and work through the catastrophic situations in your life, examine what has happened, and acknowledge how the tragedies have affected you. Only then will you be ready for God to make you a new person in Christ. "I praise you because I am fearfully and wonderfully made; your works are wonderful, I know that full well" (Psalm 139:14).

Though the path will be long and winding, you can overcome your abuse. "You will forget the shame of your youth" (Isaiah 54:4).

Faith means trusting God, even when the path before you seems insurmountable. By faith, you choose to trust Him to make the road smooth. "I will turn the darkness into light before them and make the rough places smooth. These are the things I will do; I will not forsake them" (Isaiah 42:16).

Faith in God is not just a *feeling*. It is a *knowing*. It is a decision to trust Him to work in your life. Once you make this choice, God can begin changing you. As you see healing take place in your heart and life, the fruit of faith will follow.

• "Just Forgive and Forget"

Those who do not understand the long-term effects of abuse may say that you should just "forgive and forget." This advice can be extremely detrimental because it makes you feel invalidated, as if no one is really listening to or believing your story.

You need assurance that when you take that first step of disclosing your pain to another human being, that person will believe you and be empathetic toward the feelings associated with your shocking revelation. The support you receive will encourage you to take the next step in the healing process.

A simplistic platitude such as "just forgive and forget" may cause you to retreat back into your shell of denial. You may try to forget what has happened to you, but find that it's impossible. This results in an even greater level of frustration and discouragement.

Until you go through the proper steps to recovery, you will be unable to forgive the person or persons who perpetrated the abuse. Feelings of hurt and bitterness will continue to dwell in your heart. You will berate yourself for your inability to follow such simple advice as "forgive and forget," causing your self-esteem to plummet further.

• "You Can Do This on Your Own"

Because I was born into a family that strongly encouraged self-reliance, asking for help from family, friends, or the medical community was always difficult for me, no matter what the reason. I considered it a sign of weakness. I had always taken care of my problems on my own. Pride hovered over me like a relentless cloud.

At a particular point in my life, the Lord started teaching me to let go of my proud spirit and allow others to help me in time of need. This was a continual learning process for me. "I hate pride and arrogance," God says in Proverbs 8:13. "When prides comes, then comes disgrace, but with humility comes wisdom" (Proverbs 11:2). "God will bring down their pride" (Isaiah 25:11).

People who have gone through traumatic experiences often give the appearance of being filled with pride and self-confidence. In reality, the pain of their past took away their confidence and strength. They now hide behind a facade of arrogance because they feel too vulnerable and weak to ask for help.

If your inability to trust has been destroyed, you may become consumed with controlling everyone and everything in your life in an attempt to feel safe. No one is allowed into your personal space. You fear that somehow your secrets will be disclosed, and that fear causes intense insecurity. No one could really care about you, so you become suspicious of anyone who offers you guidance and support. You say to yourself, *I'll just do it on my own. That way, no one will never know what happened to me.* You see other people who have survived various catastrophes in life and say, *If they can do it, I can too.*

But there's a big difference between surviving and truly enjoying life.

Nothing adds to the quality of life like people. You need others to validate you and love you unconditionally. To be fully enjoyed, life must include meaningful relationships. If you are filled with brokenness and pain, you will be incapable of giving or receiving love from others or even yourself.

The Risk of Being Misunderstood

Seeking help involves taking a great risk. It means removing your masks, coming out from behind imaginary walls, and making yourself vulnerable. It's an extremely frightening thing to do. But no one can help you without your permission. You have to take the risk of letting others into your life.

Unfortunately, friends, loved ones, authorities in the legal system, and even people in ministry may not be as supportive as they should be. This is not because of a lack of caring but a lack of understanding. They simply do not identify with your pain.

If a victim survives a sexual assault and presses charges, the disrespect a jury may feel toward the perpetrator is often transferred to the victim the moment she enters the courtroom and testimony begins. She is quickly judged based on her "unacceptable behaviors." Her lifestyle becomes the focus of the trial rather than the violent crime that has taken place.

A juror may enter the courtroom with preconceived ideas about what "type" of girl gets raped or physically abused. Men who abuse are well aware of this kind of stereotyping. They look for women who have been abused, or those who are homeless, runaways, or prostitutes, because "those kinds" of women rarely report assaults to the police. They don't think anyone will care or believe them.

Gwen was raped by her father and an older man who lived in her neighborhood when she was a child. Her mother emotionally and physically abused her as well.

When she tried to explain to her mother what was going on with her father and his friends, the mother replied, "You're getting what you deserve." This message was profoundly imbedded into Gwen's mind. She remained powerless and never felt she deserved anything good.

Life did not get better for her as an adult. At twenty-eight years old Gwen was the mother of four children, but had never been married. Her life was filled with drugs, alcohol, and sex. She was arrested several times for using marijuana. She struggled daily to make ends meet and provide for her children. Her jobs were always short lived because she had so many absences from work. Using drugs and alcohol often kept her from being able to get out of bed in the morning.

Gwen attended church on occasion but never felt acceptable to the "churchgoers" or to God.

Jack, a man who lived in Gwen's neighborhood, occasionally repaired her car, loaned her money to pay the rent, and watched her children when she was away from home. She finally opened up to him, telling him her horror stories of abuse and rejection by her father and mother. Gwen believed he really cared about her as a person.

When Jack began making sexual advances, Gwen felt confused because she had trusted him as a friend. However, her starved heart relished the attention.

One night Jack came over to visit. Before the evening was over, he beat and raped her repeatedly as she cried and begged him to stop.

Gwen's teenage daughter woke up during the horrendous encounter and heard the pleas for help. As she raced into her mother's room, she saw Jack escaping through an open window. After trying to calm her sobbing mother, the girl helped her get dressed and drove her to the hospital.

Not only was Gwen a victim to this perpetrator, her daughter became his indirect victim as well. The daughter's world was shattered. She no longer felt safe. Her ability to trust disintegrated.

When Gwen's case went to court, she and her attorney felt confident that Jack would be sentenced for what he had done. Instead, the focus of the case shifted to Gwen's lifestyle and she became the "bad" person who *got what she deserved*. Since Gwen had known several previous sex partners, the men and women on the jury didn't believe that she had not consented to the encounter with her neighbor.

The rapist walked away without any consequences for the crime he had committed.

Before long Gwen started responding to her pain though drugs and alcohol again.

No matter what a person's past or present life may be, no one deserves to be beaten, assaulted, raped, or forced to participate in any kind of unwanted sexual activity. Women and men who have no "sordid past" are raped and abused every day. People who commit crimes must be prosecuted to prevent these reprehensible acts from occurring again and destroying the life of another human being.

If the cycle of abuse is to be stopped, the root causes of maltreatment must be understood. Help must be offered to all those who fall victim to these crimes. Society has to become better educated regarding domestic violence, abuse, rape, and sexual harassment. Until that happens, rapists, perpetrators, and child molesters will continue to walk the streets. All children, women, and even men are potential victims of these crimes.

There will always be those who refuse to accept that sexual abuse causes severe damage because the scars are not visible to the human eye. These people don't recognize that abuse is a serious offense because the shattered remains of another person's heart, mind, and emotions cannot be easily seen. No one can begin to understand another person's pain unless he has experienced a similar situation himself.

Children face this same dilemma because society sees them as being subordinate to adults. Most people in this country are of sound moral character, so they cannot begin to fathom that an adult would molest or sexually abuse a child.

Abusers sometimes try to hide their deviant behavior by becoming volunteers or professional advocates for children's rights. They may sit on boards designed to protect and provide for children. Or they might present themselves as "perfect parents" by always being involved in their children's activities at church, school, or in the community.

The abused child may appear to be strongly attached to the abusive parent because of unclear or undefined boundaries in the relationship. The abuser may lavish gifts or freedom upon the child, or refuse to set any limits. If the abuse began at an early age, before the child's consciousness of right and wrong was established, the child would not be capable of understanding that the abuse was wrong. As the child advances in years, he becomes confused and disillusioned about the inappropriate behavior. His ability to set boundaries is weak, leaving him defenseless to painful and damaging experiences in his relationships.

Lyle was a victim of incest for years before he realized that his mother's behavior was inappropriate. He had bathed with her as a small child, but it wasn't until he was around nine that he began to feel uncomfortable with this behavior. Prior to this time, he thought her touching his genitals was necessary in order to make sure he was properly bathed.

When Lyle entered puberty and refused to bathe with her, she invited him into her bedroom, where she was scantily and seductively dressed. She made overt sexual advances toward him. Seeing her exposed adult body caused him to experience arousal, and before long they engaged in sexual activities together. His mother assured him that it was her responsibility to teach him how to be a man.

While Lyle physically enjoyed the sexual encounters, he started feeling tremendous animosity toward his mother. When he occasionally made sexual advances toward her, he found the experience gratifying yet confusing. This led him to emotions of overwhelming shame and guilt. As a means of coping, he submerged himself in alcohol and drugs.

After several years of addiction, Lyle found he could no longer deny the casualties of his abuse. He finally sought professional help and counseling. His battle to regain his life is far from over, but he is making substantial progress.

WHY A VICTIM NEEDS TO SEEK HELP

Very few victims of abuse can obtain true healing without the assistance of a professional counselor or therapist who is qualified to direct the healing process. Many times victims do not receive the help they need because the people around them do not understand what they are going through.

When I was employed as a school nurse, I met a young lady named Trina. She was a great leader and an outstanding athlete.

She was strong academically, involved in her church, and held several honors in the school. But suddenly, during her senior year, she started getting angry often and easily. She became involved with a new peer group that was heavily involved in drugs and alcohol. She started skipping school, and her grades plummeted.

Trina became the *talk* of the school but not the *concern*. No one attempted to uncover what was going on in her life. She was simply penalized for her inappropriate behavior and stripped of her honors and privileges.

What no one bothered to find out was that Trina had been date raped by a young man in her class, a boy she had always trusted. If the school officials had been more informed about the signs and symptoms of abuse, intervention could have taken place and this young lady may have been rescued from the ravages of abuse.

If your life is a constant struggle, filled with fear, conflict, and hopelessness, seek professional counseling. If your relationships are destructive, therapy can help you understand the root of your problems. A skilled therapist can assess your situation and teach you the necessary skills to successfully handle life.

No one should stay in a relationship that is abusive. If children are involved, move out immediately. There are organizations and shelters that offer housing for men, women, and children involved in domestic violence. This may involve being placed in a motel temporarily until a permanent safe place can be found.

Report any form of domestic violence or abuse involving you or your children to your local police department. They will advise you if other agencies should be involved in your case.

Seek help from someone in the mental health profession, and encourage your significant others to do the same.

Refuse to go back into the abusive relationship unless your abuser receives extensive counseling and makes the necessary changes that will provide you (and your children if you have them) safety and respect.

A counselor can help you understand the cycle of abuse and its destructive effects. This understanding will help you avoid being further victimized or becoming an abuser yourself. Without help, you will remain trapped in a victim mode. Every area of your life will be adversely affected.

Even if you are able to leave the damaging relationship and find someone who has the potential to love and respect you as you deserve, the likelihood of the new relationship being successful is nonexistent unless you have worked through your issues.

Problems associated with abuse do not just go away. You will have to work hard to overcome them. But the effort to heal is always less difficult than the struggle to survive abuse.

TREATMENT PLANNING

*M*ost often, when a hurting individual finally seeks counseling, she does not go *because* she was abused; she's noticed signs of depression, anger, fear, low self-esteem, and/or an inability to maintain meaningful relationships. She might also struggle with sexual problems or an addiction to alcohol, drugs, or some other substance or activity. Although she feels guilty for the poor choices she has made (and continues to make), she finds it impossible to break her destructive patterns of behavior. She may seek help from a pastor, counselor, or an organization such as Alcoholics Anonymous, believing that if she can learn how to handle her current problems, the effects of her past abuse will be resolved.

Unfortunately this is rarely the case. Therapy for the *symptoms* of abuse is not as effective until the *root cause* of the symptoms is identified and resolved. The abused person will go through life searching aimlessly for meaning and purpose, always feeling worthless, unloved, and hopeless.

You may not understand that your current symptoms are the result of your abuse. You don't see the connection between the trauma you suffered in the past and the pain you endure today. Feeling you have no purpose, you suffer silently, depressed and without help. You see yourself as a failure and may even wonder if you are crazy.

But you don't have to continue living in fear, frustration, and failure. With the help of a professional counselor, close friends, and/or understanding family members, you can take the following steps to break out of your world of pain and suffering into a new life of hope and healing.

STEP ONE: ACKNOWLEDGE THE ABUSE

The first step is to admit that a *crime* has been committed against you, and that you are not responsible for the abuse you have suffered. This is particularly difficult. You may feel that because you were too powerless or afraid to prevent the abusive act, you are somehow to blame for it. Instead of recognizing the abuse for what it is, you see only your own personal "weaknesses."

If you are still unsure whether or not abuse has occurred in your life, reread Chapter One.

STEP TWO: FIND THE RIGHT THERAPIST

It is vital for you to find the *right* counselor, one who has a thorough understanding of abuse and how it affects a person's body, mind, and spirit. You need and deserve help from a qualified professional who has experience dealing with abuse.

Qualified does not necessarily indicate a certain type or number of college degrees. Most counselors, like other professionals, have their personal areas of expertise. Degrees in the fields of psychology, mental health, and counseling mean very little if the counselor does not possess the specific skills needed to work with victims of abuse. Make sure the therapist you select has a solid background in working with victims who have suffered the same type of abuse you have experienced.

A skilled counselor working with abuse victims will have a solid understanding of the following:

- The type of abuse you have experienced
- The effects of that abuse
- Steps in the healing process
- Skills and techniques to assist in recovery.

The therapist must offer you a safe environment in which an atmosphere of trust and respect can develop. Effective therapy will allow you to reshape your negative experiences as you work through the traumatic events that have taken place in your life.

Keep in mind you do not have to make a long-term commitment to any therapist until you have had an opportunity to personally interview him or her. You may not be able to make this decision until you have had a few sessions.

Ask a prospective counselor what percentage of his practice involves working with victims of abuse. Have him define his personal views on your type of abuse. What can you expect in terms of recovery after going through counseling? What part will he play in the therapeutic process? What are his expectations for you?

It is important to know the therapist's style. If you are not familiar with counseling terms, request that the therapist explain them to you. Inquire about his approach in developing a treatment plan for victims of abuse. Ask about the therapeutic tools he uses. This may involve workbooks, journaling, art therapy, or support groups. Request to see any materials he might use in counseling with you.

If you will be going to court, it is important to know how familiar the therapist is with the legal system. A counselor's testimony can be crucial for a client in the courtroom. Find out how many times he has testified for clients, what issues he has addressed, and how comfortable he is in doing so. Inquire about how he plans to assist you in preparing for court. Does he appear professional and confident?

A good therapist has the following characteristics:

- Maintains confidentiality
- Is nonjudgmental
- Respects your personal beliefs and values
- Offers empathy, understanding, and support
- Does not minimize your issues
- Validates your feelings and experiences
- Offers support and guidance while encouraging self-expression and self-control
- Is a good role model
- Exemplifies honesty and integrity
- Has an emotionally stable and healthy personal life
- Encourages and supports personal growth in all areas of life
- Is confident and committed to represent you and your cause in a court of law.

You will probably never find a counselor who meets all of your expectations perfectly. I recommend making a list of what you are looking for in a therapist and circling the traits you are not willing to compromise on.

When you have a realistic list, begin the task of seeking the right counselor for you. Start by asking friends, family, your physician, or church staff members for a recommendation. If the same name is given more than once, that therapist is a good person to begin with.

What if I Wasn't Abused?

If you were not abused, even as a child, a therapist can still help you deal with other issues. You should be careful not to let a counselor lead you to believe that abuse has taken place if it hasn't. Other traumatic events can have the same effects as abuse.

Divorce, for example, is a difficult situation for everyone involved. When a marriage ends, both partners—and any children they may have—experience distressing and agonizing emotions. They may feel intense pain, betrayal, fear, rejection, and/or a loss of identity.

Death has similar consequences as well. The pain associated with the loss of a loved one can last a lifetime.

Other devastating events can also be overwhelming. The loss of a job, a friendship, or a home can have serious emotional consequences.

Most emotionally healthy individuals can overcome occurrences such as these, given sufficient time and support from family and friends. Sometimes, however, people need a little extra help, especially if more than one traumatic event occurs simultaneously.

What if I'm Unsure if I've Been Abused?

Sometimes the conscious mind becomes so overwhelmed by traumatic events, victims may bury the memories of the abuse in their subconscious where, they believe, the abuse can no longer hurt them. These people may appear to live normal, healthy lives for many years after the abuse, particularly if it was a one-time event in childhood. However, the effects of the abuse will ultimately be expressed in some negative way.

Much controversy exists over repressed memories. Scientific evidence indicates that traumatic memories are stored differently from ordinary memories.[61] During times of severe stress, the brain sedates itself with opiate-like chemicals called endorphins. These chemicals are the body's way of anesthetizing itself in order to cope with pain. Rather than keeping all aspects of an event in a cohesive fashion, the endorphins cause some memories to be stored separately from others.

If you exhibit any of the symptoms of abuse, but are unclear as to whether you have been abused, seek out a qualified counselor or therapist who can help you determine if abuse has occurred. You may have repressed the painful memories as a means of survival.

Whether or not abuse has occurred in your past, therapy can help you cope with your symptoms. A competent counselor will assist you in locating the source of your pain and direct your recovery.

Don't Wait

It is the counselor's responsibility to create and maintain a secure, nonthreatening environment that allows you freedom to disclose matters of concern as you are capable of doing so. Your job is to find a therapist who can accomplish this.

Don't allow your search for a counselor to go on for too long. Until you start working closely with a therapist on a regular basis, you will not begin the healing process necessary to live a normal, healthy, happy life.

STEP THREE: FOLLOW THROUGH

After making the decision to seek professional help, the most difficult part can be making the initial call to schedule an appointment. Adults should set up the appointment

---

[61] Diane Mandt Langberg, Ph.D., AACC Counseling Library: *Counseling Survivors of Sexual Abuse* (Wheaton, Illinois: Tyndale House Publishers, Inc.), 104.

themselves, if possible, rather than having someone else do it for them. Making the appointment personally is the first step toward breaking free from your haunting past. This commitment can be helpful in building trust in the counseling relationship.

Until you are ready to engage in therapy, healing cannot begin. Taking this initial step signifies that you see the need to be involved in counseling and are willing to face the tragic events of your life.

The first visit is usually the most stressful because you may feel extremely vulnerable discussing your most private thoughts with a stranger. Once you begin to open up, the right counselor will make you feel more comfortable as you continue to share.

If the first meeting does not go well, however, you are not obligated to return. Knowing this up front can help alleviate some of the panic feelings of making an initial appointment with a counselor.

How Can I Help a Friend?

If you are not a victim of abuse but know someone who is, you should encourage your friend to attend counseling, but do not try to force her. Usually, when someone goes to counseling because they were forced, little progress is made.

The best way to encourage someone to go for therapy is to ask her if she will attend just one session. Then she can make the decision whether or not to return for follow-up visits. Making a long-term commitment for counseling can be frightening. Agreeing to one visit is less so.

Do not assume that you are responsible for your friend's recovery and healing. The most important thing you can do is to be a good listener when she needs to talk. Be a shoulder to lean on when she feels weak, frightened, and alone. Do not feel you have to answer her questions about the abuse.

Be empathetic and caring. Love her unconditionally, even when her behavior doesn't make sense. Don't enable her to live her life as a powerless victim, but hold her accountable to her decision to heal.

STEP FOUR: DEFINE THE CLIENT/THERAPIST RELATIONSHIP

It is important that you thoroughly understand the nature of the client/counselor relationship. The American Association of Counseling provides the following guidelines: "The member must inform the client of the purposes, goals, techniques, rules of procedure, and limitations that may affect the relationship at, or before, the time that the counseling relationship is entered."[62]

You should be actively involved in the direction the counseling process takes. Make sure you are advised of your rights and responsibilities as well as how to contact the therapist's licensing board in the event your rights are violated.

Confidentiality is a key issue to be addressed before counseling begins. You must be assured that discretion will be maintained—unless you become a threat to yourself or others, or if someone is a threat to you. Without the assurance of privacy in the counseling relationship, you will feel afraid and limited in your ability to disclose the circumstances of your abuse.

The Early Sessions

In the first session, you should reveal any threatening or uncomfortable situations that might arise in the client/counselor relationship. These could include certain colloquial terms, facial expressions, body movements, or actions on the

[62] Gerald Corey, *Theories and Practice of Counseling and Psychotherapy, Third Edition* (Pacific Grove, CA: Brooks/Cole Publishing Company, a division of Wadsworth, Inc., 1986, 1982, 1977), 330.

part of the counselor (such as standing or sitting too closely to you, clenched fists, or wearing certain perfumes or colognes). If you associate any of these with your abuse, you may become re-traumatized and fearful in your therapy sessions. If this occurs, the counseling process should be delayed until changes are made and you feel safe.

Because trust was destroyed as a result of your harmful experience, sharing the details of your innermost pain will take time. Establishing trust is a process that should develop over the course of the counseling relationship. Once trust starts to build, each subsequent visit should be less uncomfortable for you.

One technique I usually use in the second or third visit with a client is allowing him to set the boundaries. I ask him to sit at the opposite side of the room. I explain that I will be walking slowly toward him, and I ask him to tell me to stop when he feels I'm getting into his "personal space." This technique allows him to feel empowered in the counseling relationship. It also gives me insight regarding how much work has to be done to create trust.

If you do not feel empowered during therapy, you will feel victimized in much the same way you were during the abuse. Therefore, it is important that you be allowed to set the pace. If you are forced to move too quickly, you may become overwhelmed and feel as though you are being taken advantage of again. This, of course, can destroy the therapeutic relationship and emotionally endanger you.

Counseling will be distressing at times. You will be challenged to acknowledge the hurt in your life. It is not uncommon for individuals to want to end counseling when this takes place. Instead, be encouraged! This is a crucial turning point in your healing process. Until you acknowledge the pain in your life, you cannot begin to heal.

STEP FIVE: BE HONEST AND OPEN

Your level of recovery and healing will be controlled by the degree of honesty shown by both you and the counselor. Issues that are hidden cannot be addressed or resolved. They will remain as buried memories of past traumatic experiences.

Allow your therapist to be totally honest with you. He will challenge you to acknowledge painful and uncomfortable memories that you have put aside, denied, or forgotten in order to survive. This acknowledgment may be frightening, but it is necessary for you to heal from the wounds of your past. You can only heal to the degree that you are willing to admit to and work through these life-shattering memories.

The following poem was written by Mary, a client of mine, after our first visit. During counseling, she revealed she had suffered years of horrendous childhood abuse and was raped as an adult. Below is her poem, printed here with her permission.

> The first time I came to your office—
> I'll never forget that day—
> My heart was beating like crazy.
> I wasn't sure I'd stay.
>
> I sat in "my" chair,
> Feet on the floor.
> I couldn't stand it.
> I nearly ran out the door.
>
> I formed an opinion as I
> Looked at your dress.
> A "Miss Goody Two Shoes,"
> Which upped my level of stress.

But somewhere in all your talking,
You said something that caught my ear.
In thirty minutes of being with me,
You knew my deepest fears.

Scared?—yes, I was,
'Cause you were able to see my soul.
The pain, the fear, the hurt—
Me, in my deep, dark hole.

So I thought,
She might be the one.
But can I trust her?
Probably not.

As if reading my mind,
You had me rate my trust.
Do you remember that?
My mind was about to bust.

Trust? What's that? I thought.
A negative score for you.
Then you smiled, leaned back,
And said, "I understand."

That's when I knew.

To see if "we" would work,
To open the door to a better life,
So I can smile once more.

STEP SIX: ESTABLISH A DIAGNOSIS

After the counseling relationship has been explained and agreed upon, the focus shifts to gaining insight into your life so the therapist can assess the emotional damage that has taken place in your life and make a diagnosis.

To do this the counselor must probe a bit, asking open-ended questions. This interview process delves into the conscious and unconscious motivations for your behavior, your strengths and weaknesses, coping strategies, the predominant defense mechanisms you use, and the conditions in which they are used. The counselor then determines what support systems and networks are available for you, your points of vulnerability, and areas of aptitude and achievement.[63]

At this point the therapist will ask specific, pointed questions about the symptoms you are having. After discussing and assessing this information, you and the counselor can begin formulating a treatment plan to facilitate your recovery.

STEP SEVEN: DEAL WITH THE ISSUES

Once a diagnosis is made, the therapist can begin guiding you in working through issues related to the abuse. These include, but are not limited to, trust, low self-esteem, guilt, shame, intimacy, anger, fear, grief, loss, powerlessness, control, forgiveness, and confronting the perpetrator in person or through role play. The counselor will assist you in replacing ineffective coping methods with positive ones. He becomes the bridge between old and new behaviors, praising you for your efforts and successes.

Because each individual is unique, there is no set pattern or time frame in working through issues related to abuse.

[63] John A. Talbott, M.D., Robert E. Hales, M.D., Stuart C. Yudofsky, M.D., eds., *The American Psychiatric Press Textbook of Psychiatry*, R. R. Donnelley & Sons Company (American Psychiatric Press, Inc. 1400 K Street N.W., Washington, DC, 1988), 164.

Therefore, it is important for you and your counselor to continually assess your progress. Goals and approaches to therapy may have to be altered from time to time in order to meet your needs.

One thing most victims of abuse have in common is an inability to see themselves as capable of being successful. As you begin to understand the trauma that has occurred in your life, you will start to make changes that will release you from the consequences of your past.

It is common for clients to fear success. Because their abusive episodes crushed their self-esteem and determination, every endeavor in life becomes a major undertaking. Frequently, just at the point of success, they will suddenly give up. The abused person feels she has given 100 percent just to make it as far as she has. She feels she has nothing left to fight with, even when the next level is close at hand.

Continuing to reach for success, even when you feel you have no "fight" left within you, will build the confidence and stamina you need to rebuild your life.

STEP EIGHT: SET GOALS

Together, you and your counselor will set goals that will lead to healing. These must be realistic and attainable. They must reflect the personal changes and accomplishments you desire and are capable of making.

A counselor can help you reach for goals and dreams you may have never before imagined. He does this by looking for strengths and potential hidden beneath your pain and insecurity.

Goals should be re-evaluated and revised when appropriate. As short-term goals are accomplished, new ones should be established that lead to the successful completion of long-term plans. If a goal becomes unachievable, or too difficult for you to accomplish at a certain stage of your recovery, it should be reevaluated and revised to eliminate the possibility of feeling like a failure. Goals are intended to enhance the healing process, not impede its progress.

One way to reach your goals may be to obtain training or education that will allow you to become independent. This will help you avoid being stuck in an abusive relationship because of your economic dependence on your abuser. A good friend or counselor can help you find ways to obtain training through a local technical school or college. Some careers have correspondence training that can be completed from your home via mail or the Internet.

If you are diagnosed with depression, or if a professional in the medical or mental health field has verified that abuse has taken place in your past, you may qualify for a disability program that offers financial aid for college or certain technical schools. The laws in each state vary, so check with your local or state agencies for details.

Achieving personal independence will free you from financial bondage to an abusive relationship and will allow you to gain the respect your abuser is unable to supply.

STEP NINE: MAKE THE DECISION TO CHANGE

It is far easier to set goals than to put them into action. Talking about ways to accomplish your dreams can be comforting, gratifying, and encouraging. However, the fear of failure can cripple you from taking even the first step toward reaching those goals.

In spite of the awful pain and torment you may carry, the decision to change is not an easy one. It requires that you leave your comfort zone, a familiar world in which you have survived for months or even years, and step out into the unknown.

This mysterious territory can be threatening and intimidating. You fear what will be expected of you. Healing means you will have to give up your masks. You must tear down the walls of protection that have allowed you to hide from the world and be excused from joining the game of life.

This venture is too terrifying to embark on alone. You must have people who will support you and encourage you when the load gets too heavy and change appears even more sinister than the abuse. Unfortunately you may feel so responsible for the pain of your loved ones that you focus all of your attention on alleviating their pain. You repress your own feelings and needs, which interferes with your recovery.

STEP TEN: ESTABLISH A SUPPORT SYSTEM

When you make the decision to change, you need to build a support system of friends and loved ones. But before they can help you rebuild your broken world, these supporters need to recognize that they have been victimized as well. Traumatic experiences inflicted on one family member permeate the entire group. When someone is abused, that person's family dynamics change dramatically. You no longer see or relate to people the way you did before the attack took place. Every relationship you have is affected.

It is important for your immediate family members to get their own individual counseling. These significant people can become emotionally and even physically exhausted if they let their fears and anxieties build. Emotionally unhealthy people are ineffective in helping others. Only after they gain some understanding of what has taken place, and begin healing from the disturbances they have encountered, can they support you in your healing process.

In counseling, family members can reach a better understanding of what you have experienced and gain insight into their own feelings as well. They can benefit greatly by discussing the losses they have sustained, or may face in the future, as a result of your abuse. Each person in your life should be encouraged to openly and honestly share his concerns and fears.

Close friends and family members of abuse victims actually go through a grieving process. Few people understand grief in terms other than physical death. But grief occurs whenever there is a loss, and both you and your family have suffered tremendous loss. Some of these losses—such as safety, trust, future plans and dreams, and the potential for meaningful relationships—may last a lifetime. Each person's individual needs must be addressed.

Parents of an abused child tend to take responsibility for what happened, even if they were unaware that abuse was taking place. They grieve deeply, believing they failed their child. A father may feel guilty because his role in the family is that of protector. The mother is considered the healer in the home, responsible for mending all the children's hurts. But abuse is an injury no father can fully protect his child from and no mother can truly fix.

Siblings are often overlooked by family members and friends during this time, but they have tremendous needs too. If no one talks about what happened to you, your brothers or sisters will interpret everyone's body language, hushed conversations, and reluctance to discuss the situation in their own way. If a police officer comes to your home as part of the investigation process, your siblings may worry that they are in trouble or being blamed for whatever has happened to you. If you go to the doctor or hospital, your brothers or sisters may worry that you are going to die. If they know you have been abused, they may worry that they will be abused as well, especially if the perpetrator has not been apprehended.

Because you will require constant care and attention, your siblings may feel neglected or abandoned. They can become jealous and may start acting out in order to gain the attention of the parents.

At some point, it will be beneficial for you to attend family counseling sessions with your loved ones. This will allow you to see that your family is committed to supporting you. In this setting, you can communicate your needs and expectations to the people in your support system. Trust starts to rebuild as you receive support, unconditional love, and acceptance from others.

Family counseling can also be a time to share happy memories of the past and hopes for the future. A positive atmosphere gives each family member a chance to share openly and honestly in a healthy environment. Family members are hurting, too, and they need to be heard and supported as well.

It is important to keep in mind that no counselor can promise a full and complete recovery to any victim of abuse. Such wounds run deep, and no matter how much healing takes place, scars will remain.

Good and Bad Support Systems

A support group should provide a safe environment for victims to share their stories of abuse and receive support from other victims they can identify with. Meeting with others who have been abused, in a place of refuge and understanding, will help you recognize the impact the traumatic events you've experienced have had on your life.

Rather than constantly focusing on the details of the abuse, competent support group leaders will challenge members to move beyond their victimization and adversities.

They will suggest that members look within themselves for inconsistencies in what they are saying and what is actually happening in their lives. Good leaders urge members to explore ways of solving their problems rather than looking for someone to rescue them.

Support groups, if not facilitated by someone who is trained in leading such gatherings, can end up encouraging negative behaviors. Participants become re-victimized when the meetings repeatedly center around members telling their stories of abuse rather than focusing on ways of overcoming the lingering effects. Negative behaviors occur when a member dominates the conversation and activities of the group. Other members may feel they are being controlled by this dominator, almost as if they are in the presence of their perpetrator. When this occurs an abused person may experience flashbacks of being powerless and controlled by their abuser.

Good facilitators recognize such happenings and carefully redirect the focus of the meetings.

Poorly organized support groups can actually add more destruction to your life. If accountability and structure are lacking, members may spend inordinate amounts of time simply comparing their stories and wounds. Each person attempts to present herself as more victimized than the others. Members make excuses for their poor choices and frequently fall back into old patterns of behavior. The group then becomes ineffective and members remain trapped in self-pity and misery.

A truly beneficial support group is actually an accountability group. The term *accountability* implies that you are responsible for your own healing, rather than expecting others to do the work for you. Sharing experiences in a healthy manner gives you a sense of identity, which allows you to feel understood because you share similar life occurrences.

As group members recover in different time frames, those who are further along in their healing can serve as an encouragement to others. Sensitive issues are addressed in a nonthreatening manner. This allows you to process what has happened to you without condemnation and move forward with the restoration of your life.

Members of an accountability group hold one another liable for the commitments they have made. Rather than making excuses, they foster honesty and facilitate trust. The group experience provides an atmosphere where emotions can be expressed in constructive and helpful ways.

Being part of a group reminds you that you are not alone. There is nothing as effective as believing someone understands what you have gone through and is willing to seek healing along with you.

If you are not currently in a supportive group, ask your therapist to assist you in finding one.

STEP ELEVEN: CHANGE

Change, whether positive or negative, can be frightening for anyone.

The axiom "Three steps forward and two steps back" is particularly true for recovering abuse victims. It is common to occasionally fall back into old patterns. The important thing is to recognize this and to continue striving for progress. Even the smallest improvements will inspire you to continue fighting the battles until the war has been won.

HEALING IS POSSIBLE

The healing process is complicated and must be achieved one step at a time. The normal activities of day-to-day life may seem like an inaccessible dream for you. Healing requires commitment, discipline, honesty, courage, and a tenacious spirit. But your past has robbed you of the emotional and physical energy needed for recovery. This is why it is vital to look for resources and people to draw strength from. You must accept help from those who are willing to aid in the rebuilding of your life.

Work on letting go of the past so you can prepare yourself for a refreshing rebirth of your heart, soul, mind, and emotions. "Forgetting what is behind and straining toward what is ahead, I press on toward the goal to win the prize for which God has called me heavenward in Christ Jesus" (Philippians 3:13–14 NIV).

MAKING RADICAL CHANGES: LOOKING WITHIN

*Y*ou've made the decision to heal, and your support systems are in place. Now you can begin the process of changing: from being a victim to becoming a survivor. To accomplish this, you must develop an entirely new belief system. Old ways of thinking and behaving must be replaced with healthy methods of making deliberate choices so you don't fall back into victimization.

You must believe that you can heal. However, since your ability to process life events is so distorted by the perpetrator's control of your mind, you will most likely need the help of your friends and family, and possibly a qualified professional counselor, to implement the steps necessary for healing. As you take each step, utilize the resources of your counselor and support people as much as necessary to accomplish these important tasks.

FACE YOUR FEARS

Most people who have endured traumatic episodes in their past become emotionally detached to escape the pain. If they occasionally experience strong feelings, they become frightened and quickly "shut down" to regain control and feel safe again.

Until you come out from behind the walls of denial and acknowledge your fears, you will continue to be controlled by your perpetrator. Giving up your defense mechanism of denial forces you to deal with the losses brought about by abuse. This may be an agonizing experience, but it is your only hope of escape from a destructive pattern of life.

Often, when I counsel an individual who has been abused, she will acknowledge feelings of depression, anger, fear, and low self-esteem. But when I ask her to tell me how she has been affected by the horrifying experiences of her abuse, she will usually deny the connection. "It hasn't affected me at all," she will say. "I honestly don't know why I feel the way I do."

Facing the disturbing recollections of your past and reconnecting to your emotions is one of the most frightening aspects of making the decision to heal. At times the pathway to healing will evoke dark and chilling memories. Unpleasant flashbacks and old, gnawing feelings that have been buried for months or even years will emerge from the deepest parts of your heart and soul. At this point you may decide that the work required to recover is just too hard. You might feel too weak and want to give up. You may believe it is easier to live with the abuse than to try to conquer it. You could resign yourself to the fact that the abuse will always have control over your life.

As frightening as it may be to begin your healing journey, this all-consuming terror can become the catalyst to restore your shattered life and world. You can exchange your terror for a sense of empowerment as you evoke your right to heal.

RESTRUCTURE YOUR THINKING

Many survivors delay their healing due to faulty thought processes. Albert Ellis's "rational-emotive therapy" model can be quite effective in restructuring your mind-set about life events in ways that allow you to avoid a life of defeat. "People have the capacity to change their cognitive, emotive, and behavioral processes," Ellis states. "They can choose to react differently from their usual patterns, refuse to allow themselves to become upset, and train themselves so that they can eventually remain minimally disturbed for the rest of their life."[64]

I have found this to be especially true in working with victims of abuse. By consciously changing your thought patterns from internalized messages of degradation and despair to empowering messages of courage and hope, you can conquer the fears and obstacles that are blocking your way to a new life: a life free from constant pain and self-destructive behaviors.

A great majority of the clients I see in my practice also have physical conditions that create stress and pain in their lives. There is a definite connection between mind and body.

Thoughts are just one part of our body's wisdom. A thought held long enough and repeated enough becomes a belief. The belief then becomes biology. If we don't work through our emotional distress, we set ourselves up for physical distress because of the biochemical effect that suppressed emotions have on our immune and endocrine systems.[65]

Proverbs 18:21 says, "Death and life are in the power of the tongue, and those who love it will eat its fruit" (NASB). The Message translates this verse, "Words kill, words give life; they are either poison or fruit—you choose." We speak what we think. Life is filled with unpleasant experiences, and everyone is adversely affected by traumatic experiences.

However, you can choose how those experiences will affect you. You don't have to live your life in hopelessness. You can choose to be set free from the past by what you decide to believe and do about your future. You have the freedom to choose life or death. Choose life!

64   Gerald Corey, *Theory and Practice of Counseling and Psychotherapy, Third Edition* (Brooks/Cole Publishing Company, a division of Wadsworth, Inc., Pacific Grove, CA, 1986), 211.

65   Christine Northrup, M.D., *Women's Bodies, Women's Wisdom: Creating Physical and Emotional Health and Healing* (Bantam Books, New York, 1994).

REDUCE AREAS OF STRESS

Your body has gone through tremendous stress and strain as your mind has attempted to cope with the traumatic experiences in your past. The following suggestions will help you alleviate controllable stressors in your life and enhance your rate and level of success as you strive for emotional healing.

- **Take responsibility for your life.** Don't wait for someone else to rescue you and make your life better. Until you become confident and secure in who you are, you will live in a repeated cycle of victimization and will never experience life as a survivor. Confidence comes from engaging in relationships and activities that challenge you to push beyond your comfort zone. Personal strengths will emerge that will empower you to accomplish tasks you never dreamed were possible to achieve. This newly discovered self-assurance will enhance your assertiveness skills. These in turn will equip you to take responsibility for your life.

- **Exercise.** Any physical activity, even walking, greatly reduces stress and adds to your total well-being. To obtain optimal healing, you must strive to function at peak performance in every area of your life. Exercising renews your body and mind. This equips you to deal with the challenges before you. Studies have shown that exercise has the following benefits:[66]

  1. Lower cancer rates and better immune system function

---

[66] Christine Northrup, M.D., *Women's Bodies, Women's Wisdom: Creating Physical and Emotional Health and Healing* (Bantam Books, New York, 1994).

2. A life expectancy that is, on average, seven years longer

3. Less depression and anxiety, and better mental efficiency and speed

4. More relaxation, assertiveness, spontaneity, and enthusiasm; greater self-acceptance and a better attitude about one's body

5. Stronger bones, increased bone thickness, increased bone mass, and increased ability of the bone to resist mechanical stress and fracture

6. More restful sleep

7. Higher self-esteem

Before starting a rigorous exercise program, always check with your physician.

- **Get organized.** Set your priorities. Make a daily schedule that enables you to accomplish your objectives and goals, and stick to it as much as possible without allowing it to become another area of stress. Don't commit yourself to more obligations and responsibilities than you can handle.

- **Don't rush.** You won't accomplish much if you're so stressed out that you become unhealthy mentally, emotionally, or physically. When you start feeling stress, change your activity. If stress continues to mount, take a break and relax.

- **Understand your limitations**. Recognize your talents and gifts, your strengths and weaknesses. Don't force yourself to take on tasks you are not qualified to do, you don't have the skills to perform well, or you simply don't have the time for. You shouldn't be ashamed to acknowledge and express areas of your life where you lack expertise. Taking on too many duties can be overwhelming and will result in added stress. Learning to say no may be one of your greatest stress relievers.

- **Accept reality.** Realize that there are certain situations you can't change; don't waste your time and energy trying to change those things. Fighting the impossible will only stress you out. Remember the Serenity Prayer: *God grant me the serenity to accept the things I cannot change, the courage to change the things I can, and the wisdom to know the difference.* Amen!

- **Make relaxation time**. Find time to engage in activities that bring you pleasure and relaxation. Allow yourself time for meditation and prayer, reflecting back on the day's occurrences, or looking forward to future events. Visit with family and friends. If you aren't accustomed to relaxing, you may want to start this new discipline by setting aside five minutes for inactivity. Gradually increase the time.

As you work toward emotional and mental healing, do your best to maintain the highest possible degree of health in all areas of your life—mental, emotional, physical, and spiritual.

CHANGE YOUR DIET

If you have never paid much attention to the way you eat, this would be a good time to make a personal assessment of your nutritional needs. I am not implying that if you maintain a healthy diet, you will not be affected by abuse or other traumas. But a well-nourished body will be much better equipped to handle stressful situations. Our minds must be properly nourished in order to think clearly and make good decisions.

Most people's standard diet consists mainly of high-fat and highly processed junk foods that offer little, if any, nutritional value. The farmland our foods are grown in has been contaminated by fertilizers and pesticides. The air we breathe and the water we drink are chemically contaminated. Our bodies can go into chemical overload from constant exposure to these toxic chemicals.

Depression, anxiety, and low self-esteem are common symptoms of abuse or other emotionally traumatic experiences. These same symptoms, however, may also result from a poor diet or a chemically toxic environment. A healthy diet has the potential to help you maintain a healthy outlook on life. This will make you better able to process the emotions related to your abuse.

Sweets can cause depression, anxiety, and other negative emotions due to rapid shifts in blood-sugar levels. "Most people can handle the stresses of ordinary life if they eat properly. When blood sugar rises because of the ingestion of a quick sugar (table sugar, brown sugar, corn syrup, maple syrup, honey), the pancreas responds by producing insulin, perhaps more than is necessary. Down plummets the blood sugar and a number of responses, usually mental, are produced."[67]

Eat a balanced diet consisting of fresh fruits and vegetables, grains, meats, dairy products, nuts, and seeds (taking into consideration any allergies or other health problems you may have). Drink plenty of water.

Consult with your physician if you have a health condition that could be adversely affected by a diet change. You might consider a consultation with a licensed dietician or nutritionist who is qualified to evaluate your dietary needs.

---

[67] Lendon Smith, M.D., *Feed Yourself Right* (Dell Publishing Co., Inc., New York, 1983).

Check with your local hospital or health care facility to locate one in your area. Try to find a nutritionist or dietician who takes a holistic approach to health. Not only do they recommend a balanced diet, they also understand the harmful, damaging effects of "junk foods."

Work toward keeping your diet and your environment as clean and chemical free as possible. Reducing exposure to toxic chemicals can be an immense task. Listed below are exposures that are most controllable. This is a good place to start in protecting your physical condition, which in turn affects your mental/emotional health.

- Eat organically grown, chemical-free foods that have not been processed.

- Drink purified or natural/spring bottled water.

- Avoid using pesticides, cleaning supplies, and personal-care products that are laden with noxious chemicals. Be informed about toxic chemicals and learn to read labels on products. You can do this by visiting the health section of your bookstore or your local health food store. Or arrange for an appointment with a physician or clinic that specializes in environmental health. There are also several Web sites that provide information on the dangers of chemicals. For example: Resources for the Chemically Injured, Chemically Sensitive or Environmentally Ill (www.snowcrest.net/lassen/mcsei.html), The Chemical Injury Information Network (www.ciin.org), and The Edelson Center for Environmental and Preventive Medicine (www.ephca.com). Do a search for "Chemical Sensitivity" for additional Web sites.

- Avoid spending time in buildings and facilities that have a toxic environment. This includes workplaces where products are manufactured using toxic chemicals, as well as homes (including mobile homes) that have been built or manufactured quite recently. Many people have become extremely ill because the building materials used in their homes or workplaces are loaded with chemicals. This is sometimes known as "sick building syndrome."

REPROGRAM PARENTAL MESSAGES

Parents are a child's most important role models. They instilled the values, morals, beliefs, and attitudes you carried into adulthood. Their lives gave you a foundation upon which to design and build your own life. They taught you how to relate to others by the way they treated you, each other, and other family members.

When mothers and fathers are in constant conflict, children have a tendency to think their parents' attitudes and actions are a direct response to their bad behavior. This faulty thinking says, *"If I wasn't such a bad child, they wouldn't have to act that way."*

Sometimes the need to stay in an unhealthy lifestyle comes from being raised in a home where one or both parents were abusive, and the abuser never took responsibility for his malicious actions.

DEAL WITH THE GRIEF

As you begin to face your fears, restructure your thinking patterns, and re-program the damaging parental messages you have received, the next step in your recovery is to acknowledge and work through your grief.

You have experienced the loss of some very important things such as trust, honor, respect, relationships, power, security, self-esteem, and hope. Once you acknowledge your losses, you can begin to work through the various stages of grief.

• **Shock and Disbelief**. As you become aware of all that has been stolen from you, you will experience shock and disbelief. At times you may even convince yourself that the abuse never took place. In the past, you may have been able to acknowledge a void in your life, but until now, you never associated those feelings of emptiness with a crime committed against you. To prevent emotional overload, you may need to take several weeks to work through this initial stage. You may have to grieve each loss separately. Allow yourself adequate time to do so. No one else should be permitted to set the pace for you.

• **Anger.** If you were raised in a home where expressing anger was considered bad or unacceptable, admitting anger can be frightening. It reinforces what your abuse made you feel about yourself. While experiencing anger is necessary in recovering from abuse, it has the potential to inflict further pain on your life if it is not dealt with and expressed in healthy ways. If you are not careful, you may find yourself venting your anger on anyone who is connected to your perpetrator, or toward family members or others you thought should have protected you.

Feelings of anger may be vented in several self-destructive ways: outwardly, as rage; inwardly, in the form of depression; or in passive-aggressive ways. If you cope with anger by raging, you may alienate your much-needed support system by physically, mentally, or emotionally attacking them. Because the people in your support system do not understand your behavior, they may withdraw in order to protect themselves. To prevent this, take the following steps:

1. Identify the source of your anger. Until you understand the reason for your rage, it will remain unmanageable. It will control your life, causing you to act in ways that bring more misery and isolation.

To escape the consequences of your fury, you must name your perpetrator. Many victims are too fearful to even mention their abuser's name. Place yourself in a safe environment. You may want to begin by writing the perpetrator's name on a piece of paper until you reach a point in recovery where speaking his name is no longer threatening to your psychological well-being.

2. Talk about your anger. Verbalizing your anger puts it into proper perspective. Reflect on your words and make the decision to begin the process of letting it go. Talking about your anger can also provide your support system with insight into your chaotic life and the many effects the abuse has had on it.

3. Keep a journal. Journaling allows you to express your pain without the fear of being misunderstood, judged, or rejected. It places you in a position of power over your abuser, as it affords you the luxury of addressing the perpetrator and the pain he inflicted in your life without the fear of further violence and abuse. Journaling allows you to reach into your soul and touch base with your emotions in a safe environment.

4. Engage in physical activity. Walking, running, exercising, or hitting a punching bag are great ways to release frustration. This prevents the anger from building and turning into rage. Using the punching bag as a substitute for your abuser can be a very rewarding experience. It symbolically allows you to inflict pain on your perpetrator without fear of repercussion.

5. Take an anger management class. Community resource centers often provide these classes through individual and group counseling services. This type of course will teach you how to control or eliminate your anger in a safe, nondestructive manner.

• **Bargaining.** This stage occurs when you feel helpless and start looking for a possible solution to your loss. You may bargain with God, making promises to Him if He will only make the pain go away. Bargaining can be useful in processing grief because it allows you time to see your situation as it really is. Unfortunately this step may lead you to believe that you don't have to work through the remaining stages of your grief, because you have made an agreement with God. Do not allow your grief work to stop at this stage. Much is to be gained by persevering and moving closer to recovery.

• **Guilt.** Guilt results from faulty thinking that says, "Somehow I caused this pain in my life" or "I should have been able to stop it." You must correct this thought process by placing blame where it belongs—on the abuser. Remind yourself of the powerless state you were in when you were abused. You were helpless and unable to do anything about what was happening to you. If you were a child when the abuse took place, see the abuse through the eyes of a child rather than the adult you are now. Ask yourself if you would ever judge a child guilty for abuse that occurred in her life. Grant yourself this same respect and honor.

• **Depression.** It is natural to feel sad about the abuse that has taken place and how much it has taken away from you. But if you fall into a depressed state for a prolonged period of time, you may become immobilized by hopelessness and fear. This will delay the healing process or may even stop it altogether. If you feel suicidal or stuck in depression, seek professional counseling and schedule an appointment with your physician. After evaluating your condition, your doctor may prescribe an anti-depression medication that you can take while focusing with your counselor on ways to work through and eliminate the depression. Anti-depressants can help you escape your state of hopelessness, helping you pull together your emotional resources to acknowledge and work through your losses.

• **Acceptance.** Your goal is to ultimately reach the stage of acceptance when you realize that although you can do nothing to change what has happened, you can choose to move from being a victim to becoming a survivor. The time involved in reaching this stage varies. You can tell that you have reached this stage if you can:

1. Talk about the abuse without feeling victimized again.
2. Connect emotionally with yourself, other people, and the world around you.
3. Eliminate unhealthy coping patterns, habits, and relationships from your life.
4. Live your life outside the control of the abuse or the perpetrator of that abuse.
5. Live life in the present and look forward with anticipation to the future.

AVOID OBSESSIVE RESPONSIBILITY FOR OTHERS

You are not responsible for the happiness and welfare of the people in your life. Many victims of abuse, believing that their own problems are too big to fix, subconsciously choose to rescue others whose problems seem minor in comparison.

Rescuing someone else allows the abused person to temporarily escape their pain and fear. They feel they can achieve success by tackling these smaller problems. Unfortunately, this rarely happens because the helper lacks the skills and strength necessary to be an effective support person.

To truly help another person, you must be healthy and strong—mentally, emotionally, and spiritually. Do not spend all of your time trying to rescue another person when you desperately need to rescue yourself.

ASSIGN BLAME WHERE BLAME IS DUE

Victims of abuse often develop a distorted pattern of thinking that makes them feel responsible for the abuse they suffered. This misshapen view of what has taken place in your life may be self-imposed from the trauma, or may result from other people you come in contact with. Too often, family members who are angry about what has taken place, yet feel powerless to do anything about it, will transfer their anger onto the victim, blaming her for the assault.

When Roxanne was a seventeen-year-old senior in high school, her strict parents instituted an 11:00 curfew. One night she went to a party that her parents approved of because it was chaperoned by responsible adults.

As the time for her curfew approached, Roxanne called her parents to ask that her curfew be extended until midnight. Her father, who was never flexible with schedules, refused her request.

"But I'm always home on time," Roxanne argued. "You're being unfair."

Her father would not budge.

A male friend, whom Roxanne had always respected and enjoyed being around, overheard the conversation and came up with a plan. Roxanne drove herself home in time to meet her curfew, then went into her parents' bedroom and told them she was home and was going to bed. Fifteen minutes later, she snuck out her bedroom window and left with the young man. Unfortunately they never made it back to the party. He took her to a remote area where he beat and raped her, recreating a scenario from a pornographic Web site he frequently viewed. When he took her home, he threatened to harm her if she ever told anyone what happened.

Terrified, and needing to be comforted and taken to the hospital for medical help, Roxanne awakened her parents and told them what had happened. Her father's first words were, "Well, you got what you deserved for sneaking out and disobeying me."

Roxanne's mother insisted on taking her to the emergency room, but her father refused to accompany them. "I'm not about to go anywhere with *her*," he said.

For Roxanne, this verbal abuse was almost as destructive as the physical assault. Her father's message was identical to her perpetrator's: *You are worthless, and my needs are more important than yours.* His words confirmed her emotional response to the beating and rape: *I am a bad person and responsible for what has happened to me.* Both her father and her attacker had an obsessive need to be powerful and in control.

Roxanne's father's message became deeply imbedded into her psyche. His caustic words severely complicated her recovery.

One of the most important steps in your healing process is to recognize that the fault lies solely with the perpetrator, not you. No one "deserves" to be abused.

When you were being abused, the perpetrator may have threatened to harm you or someone you loved if you disclosed the abuse. This veil of secrecy communicated to you that you were "bad" because you participated in such a bad thing. If the abuse took place in your childhood, this message will continue on into adulthood. As unhealthy as it is, you

177

will seek out people who allow you to recreate similar scenarios, playing the only role you know how to play—that of the bad and irresponsible person.

FORGIVE THE ABUSER

This step may seem confusing if you don't understand the true meaning of forgiveness. According to Webster's dictionary, *forgive* means "to cease to feel resentment against (an offender): pardon one's enemies; to give up resentment or a claim to requital for an insult; to grant relief from payment of a debt.[68]

Forgiveness does *not* imply that what your abuser did to you was acceptable, nor does it mean that you will forget what was done to you.

When you forgive, you choose to stop letting the abuse you suffered control your life. You make the decision to let go of the anger, bitterness, fear, pain, and the need for retaliation that have consumed your thoughts and emotions, leaving you little time for healing and moving on with your life.

Merle Shain says, in *Hearts that We Broke Long Ago,* "When you forgive, you take your enemy's power over you away, you defang them and change the atmosphere between you from highly charged to neutral, and sometimes even to rosy hued. And people, who had the power to control you just by being, can no longer command your emotions, or suck you into the vortex with a word. They cease to be the eye of your storm, and once you forgive them, they become people like any other, human and flawed, misguided on occasion, and hence rather like the rest of us."[69]

Forgiveness will take place on your timetable. However, don't let the false sense of empowerment and control that comes with an unforgiving attitude leave you trapped in a

[68]   G. & C. Merriam Company, Springfield, Massachusetts, 1977.

[69]   Merle Shain, *Hearts that We Broke Long Ago* (Bantam Books, New York, 1985).

pit of darkness and despair. Choosing to begin the process of forgiving is a positive step toward freedom and healing. The person who forgives is, in reality, bigger and more powerful than the abuser who committed the violent act.

When you choose to forgive, you no longer consider your abuser indebted to you. No amount of compensation could ever make up for the damage that has been done in your life anyway. There is no act of contrition or financial restitution that can take away your pain. Only you have the power to do that.

The person who traumatized you may lack the strength and courage to face the crime he is responsible for. But you can move beyond your trauma-filled life. Praise yourself for your bravery and determination. Your efforts will be rewarded.

EMPOWER YOURSELF

In the past, as memories flooded your mind and emotions, you quickly sought ways to find comfort and relief. Unfortunately that comfort was often obtained through harmful means. You then reverted to ineffective coping mechanisms, perhaps even drugs and alcohol.

The old thought patterns told you that you deserved abuse and pain. You must redirect your faulty thinking from familiar, negative statements to new, self-empowering ones. Tell yourself what you would like to believe about yourself. It is not what happens to us that determines the outcome of our lives, but what we tell ourselves about what has taken place. We can choose to live in victory or defeat. Choose victory.

This is a critical step in the recovery process, yet it is frequently where the victim feels so overwhelmed that she is unable to continue. At this juncture it is vital that you reach out to your support system instead of returning to your past ways of coping. If you don't, you will abandon your plans for healing and re-enter a life of repeated victimization and abuse.

REWARD YOURSELF

Find ways to reward yourself for achieving your goals. Stand in front of a mirror and praise yourself. Record the milestones in a journal where you can read about them from time to time. Share your accomplishments with a support person who will affirm you. Such activities can be very empowering, encouraging you to take the next difficult step.

When Suzanne finally got the nerve to tell her abusive husband she was filing for divorce because she could no longer tolerate his control and emotional abuse, she began making plans to attend college. She had always wanted to obtain a college degree, but her husband always told her that he was the only one in the family who needed an education. Suzanne had never been allowed to work outside the home. This kept her dependent on her spouse and gave him even greater control in their relationship. Now, things were going to change.

Suzanne called a friend who was attending college and made plans to meet on campus the next day so the friend could help her apply for admission. The two young ladies cried and laughed together as they celebrated Suzanne's decision to break free from her abusive past.

The day after Estelle, a twenty-eight-year-old single woman, finally got up the nerve to tell her abusive boyfriend to leave their shared apartment, she immediately called several family members and friends and invited them to dinner the next night. She then drove to the employment agency and applied for a job. Next she went to the bank and opened her own checking account for the first time in her life.

Over the ensuing months, Estelle felt a sense of pride and independence as she launched a new career and gained control over her finances. Her self-esteem soared as she experienced validation from the wise decisions she made.

Both Suzanne and Estelle celebrated when they made the decision to heal, reached out for support, and chose to change their destructive ways of thinking.

Praise yourself for your efforts, even when they are not completely successful. Without effort, goals are never accomplished.

REFUSE TO TURN BACK

You must decide that in spite of your pain, you cannot return to your old patterns of behavior. Going back to familiar habits is easy to do. You must be diligent in working through your recovery.

Come up with a "Crisis Plan" that you can use in the event you feel vulnerable to your old patterns of coping. Make a list of people you can call during these times and keep their phone numbers in a handy place. Sign an accountability contract with a support person, indicating that you will call them, or a backup person if they are unavailable, during times of crisis. This will provide you with a sense of safety and predictability as you face your pain-ridden past.

When you feel weak, frightened, or hopeless, remember to seek the true source of strength. "I can do all things through Christ who strengthens me" (Philippians 4:13 NKJV).

MAKING RADICAL CHANGES: REACHING OUT

*Y*ou must now examine various aspects of your life and determine to make whatever adjustments are necessary to lead you to recovery. Radical changes may have to be made in order to reshape your world and allow you to enter into healthy, rewarding relationships.

RELEASE THE SECRET

Finally letting go of your dark, long-held secrets is an extremely frightening venture. You are taking an enormous risk of being rejected or misunderstood. However, continuing to live in secrecy will only increase your feelings of shame and guilt. It will keep you isolated, left alone to carry this heavy burden. Until you talk to someone about what happened, real healing can never take place.

Abuse is most difficult to report when incest is involved. The thought of telling anyone that you have been sexually involved with a family member is humiliating.

Whether you were abused by a family member, friend, or stranger, it is important to remind yourself that you are not responsible for what this person has done to you. He has stolen enough from you already. Don't let him rob you of your hope for healing by continuing to live with this ugly secret.

No matter what form of abuse you have suffered, do not let the fear of being disbelieved keep you silent. Continue telling your story until someone believes you. It may be difficult for those who love you to hear about the details of your abuse. They will be battling a multitude of emotions themselves, so you may receive a number of different responses. They might become hostile and aggressive, or withdrawn and sad. Allow them to discuss their feelings with you, whatever those feelings might be. However, be careful not to fall back into old habits of protecting others, even your supporters, by holding yourself responsible for their emotions.

Talking about your abuse may provide the encouragement necessary for others to disclose abuse that has occurred in their lives as well. This kind of sharing will give both of you a sense of being understood. You can support and encourage each other during this difficult time. No longer will you feel alone and different.

Sharing the secret of abuse will be a great relief. A heavy load will be lifted, making the journey to healing easier. Don't feel you have to talk about all the gory details of the abuse with everyone. Share only what you are comfortable with. With the passing of time, you may feel more at ease giving an extensive account of what happened. You have the right to determine when you will share your story and with whom. No one should make that decision for you.

The people you tell can become your best supporters as you give them permission to be involved in your recovery. Let them know how they can help you, but don't expect them to do your healing for you. Only you have the power and ability to do that.

Informing family and friends of your decision to heal places you in a position of accountability to them. Once you share your story, you can no longer deny that the abuse occurred.

Don't be afraid to set limits and boundaries with those to whom you have chosen to be accountable. Do not allow them to overprotect you or discourage you from growing and moving on. Here are some examples of how this might occur:

- Trying to keep you from going to counseling in order to prevent you from having to deal with unpleasant memories.

- Not allowing you time alone for fear that someone else might harm you.

- Discouraging you from speaking out about your abuse.

- Trying to compensate for your losses by doing everything for you.

Do not let your supporters minimize your abuse by telling you that:

- Bad things are a normal part of life, and you should just get over it.

- It's only as bad as you allow it to be.

- The abuse only lasted for a short period of time, so it shouldn't affect you for a lifetime.

- You really shouldn't talk about it because if you do, you will never get over it.

- The abuse would never have happened if you had not been a weak, dependent person.

If the above comments are directly or indirectly made to you, do not hesitate to correct the person making such erroneous statements.

CONFRONT THE PERPETRATOR

A time may come when you will want to confront your perpetrator. The decision to do so can be both frightening and empowering. Do not let anyone force or convince you to deal with him unless you are ready, and can do so without any preconceived ideas or expectations.

Before you decide to contact or meet with your perpetrator, you must determine your reasons for doing so. Do you want:

- To express and release anger?

- To regain power and control?

- To seek retribution?

- To assign responsibility for the abuse to the attacker?

When you confront your abuser, try not to have any unrealistic expectations. Perpetrators usually show little if any remorse. Prepare yourself for all possible responses. If your abuser does not seem the least bit repentant, how will you respond to that disappointment?

Your purpose for confronting should be to reverse the power in the relationship. Your presence and message should convey to him that he will never control or abuse you again. Once you make the decision to confront, make sure you do so in a safe environment.

If you have reported the abuse to the legal system, check to see if your state offers "Victim's Empathy." If so, your legal representatives will make arrangements for you to face the perpetrator in a protected setting. You will be able to choose those you would like have in the room while the confrontation takes place. The perpetrator will be encouraged to answer your questions, but you will probably never hear all that you hope to.

If you decide to challenge your abuser outside the court system, make sure you are surrounded by a strong group of supporters both during the confrontation and for an extended time afterward.

Carefully consider whether a personal confrontation is more likely to enhance your healing, destroy it, or delay it. As an alternative to the direct approach, many survivors choose to confront their perpetrators through letter writing, phone calls, or by using drama and role playing, either privately or in therapy.

EVALUATE YOUR LIFE

As recovery begins, examine every area of your life to determine which ones need to be changed. Which people and things have a positive effect on you, and which have an adverse or negative effect? Evaluate each person and situation on an individual basis. If a relationship or situation does not enhance your healing, it should be ended or at least temporarily disrupted.

This evaluation could be difficult because of the state of confusion you have been in. You may need to seek counsel from a therapist, trusted friend, or pastor.

If abuse involving family members has taken place, you must determine if it is healthy for you to be around or exposed to the perpetrator. Because *nobody understands your pain*, family members may expect you to simply forgive the perpetrator and forget the past so the family will not be disrupted any more than necessary.

If being in the presence of your abuser makes you feel powerless and afraid, do not hesitate to refuse to be involved in family activities where he will be present. Even if he has made some sort of apology, do not feel guilty for refusing to engage in family gatherings. Just seeing the perpetrator, or even hearing his name, is likely to trigger old memories and feelings that could cause you to emotionally relive the abuse.

SET GOALS

One of the most important things you can do to heal from the past is to make new plans for your life. If you have a low self-concept or feel emotionally distraught, begin by setting short-term goals. You can establish long-term plans as you begin to heal.

Your goals may include:

- Getting in touch with your mind, body, and emotions
- Going for counseling
- Completing assignments given in therapy
- Joining a support group
- Enlisting an accountability partner
- Choosing to live life one day at a time (or even moment by moment)
- Participating in life around you
- Seeking God for strength and wisdom.

KEEP YOURSELF SAFE

You may find it necessary to move to a new place of residence. If family members or friends cannot provide a safe place for you to stay, you may seek temporary shelter in a home for battered and abused victims. These shelters employ staff members who are trained in providing emotional support as well as a secure location during this vulnerable time.

If you feel the need to protect yourself in this way, look in the Yellow Pages under SHELTERS–ABUSED PERSONS & CHILDREN. There you will find a toll-free telephone number and possibly a local number. The phones are answered twenty-four hours a day, seven days a week.

You will notice that the phone book does not list an address. The locations of these facilities are not disclosed to the public for the safety of the victims seeking sanctuary there.

If you cannot find a phone number for a local shelter, or if you are in an urgent situation that does not allow you to take the time to look up the number, you can always call 911.

PROTECT YOUR CHILDREN

People often say that children are resilient, able to bounce back from the tragedies of life. Sometimes, however, what is seen as "resilience" is simply stuffing emotions inside so they can go about their daily lives. Given time, they will exhibit behaviors that reveal their pain and anger.

Observe your children closely for signs of abuse. If you have the slightest doubt as to whether or not abuse has occurred, seek professional help for your child immediately.

The most common signs of abuse in children include:

- A sudden change in behavior

- Nightmares/night terrors (about people, snakes, spiders, monsters, etc.)

- Anger/rage (toward adults, children, or animals)

- Depression

- Withdrawal

- Lack of trust

- Control issues

- Defiance and refusal to comply with rules and requests

- Phobias/fears of people, places

- Sexually acting out with younger children, animals, or dolls

- Changes in school performance

- Refusing to sleep in his/her bedroom

- Lying, stealing, setting fires

- Becoming sexually precocious

- Enuresis and encopresis (urinating or defecating in underwear).

Typical signs of abuse in adolescents include:

- Eating Disorders (weight gain or loss)

- Depression

- Running away

- Promiscuity

- Drug and/or alcohol abuse

- Mistrust

- Dressing seductively or over-modestly

- Self-hate

- Anger/rage

- Nightmares/night terrors

- Control—either controlling or being controlled

- Defiant behavior

- Change in friends

- Change in school performance.

Just because someone exhibits one or more of the above symptoms, that does not necessarily indicate that she has been abused. The individual should be referred to a physician or qualified mental health professional for an assessment.

If you suspect a child is being abused in any way, report your suspicions immediately to your local police or call the ChildHelp USA® National Child Abuse Hotline at 1-800-4-A-CHILD® (1-800-422-4453).

Your Past Affects Their Present

Your past abusive relationships may result in a tendency to overprotect your children. It is important to avoid teaching your children to live in fear, thus making them unable to trust people.

However, do not assume that just because your abuse happened years ago, your perpetrator has stopped his immoral and destructive behaviors. If your perpetrator is still in your life, do not leave your child alone with him. Teach her to trust discriminately. Things that adults might see as normal or insignificant incidents can have disastrous, destructive effects in the life of a child.

Casey was a handsome, thirteen-year-old male whose mother brought him to me for counseling. She reported that he was a constant problem at home and school. He often exploded with anger and flew into fits of rage, refusing to comply with people in authority, especially men. His grades were failing. He had little regard for his curfew or other family rules. He had been in trouble with the legal system because of drugs and alcohol.

Casey spent little time with his father due to his dad's heavy work schedule. His mother and teachers assumed the father's absence was the cause of Casey's defiance.

After several sessions with Casey, I realized that his behavior was more than the result of "absent-father syndrome." I began to probe for possible abuse.

I asked Casey if there was anyone he would not feel safe being left alone with. He started cracking his knuckles and clearing his throat. Then he said, "Yes. My grandfather."

When I asked Casey to help me understand his fears, he began to cry. He reported that from the time he was about five years old until the age of eleven, his paternal grandfather sexually and physically abused him. After the beatings, his grandfather sometimes put a pillow over Casey's face. The grandfather told him that if he reported the beating, he would keep the pillow over his face until he suffocated to death.

I reminded Casey of my limits to confidentiality, informing him that I would have to report this to his mother, his father, and the legal system. I asked Casey how he felt about me reporting the abuse. He replied, "I'm afraid no one will believe me. They never do. They always think that I cause all the problems. My dad thinks my grandpa is perfect. I'll be in big trouble if they don't believe me."

When Casey's father and mother joined us in session, I encouraged him to describe his grandfather's abuse in his own words. The pain in Casey's eyes as he told his story took away any doubt the parents might have had. When Casey asked his dad if he believed him, tears filled the father's eyes. "Yes, Son," he said, "I believe you. That's the same thing he did to me for years. I was afraid he might abuse you, too, but I hoped he had changed. I guess I was wrong. I'm so sorry."

Never assume that an abuser has stopped his destructive behavior just because he is no longer traumatizing you. Do not believe that he has stopped just because he is elderly. No matter what the age or circumstances, report the abuse immediately.

MAKE NEW FRIENDS

It is important to place yourself in the midst of individuals who model healthy relationships. You can make such relationships through civic gatherings, church activities, accountability groups, or by connecting with couples and individuals who encourage a sense of value, worth, and personal growth within their families and friendships.

Avoid the tendency to associate with other victims who might discourage you or pull you back into dangerous situations. Even if these people have left their abusive relationships, they may lack the courage or discipline to work through the pain inflicted in their lives. Those who are weak tend to seek out other weak individuals to connect with. The pain they share gives them a sense of belonging as they bond through exchanging their nightmarish experiences.

This type of relationship gives an illusion of power because you both feel connected and understood. But the lack of discipline you share will keep both of you powerless, trapped in a world of dysfunction and abuse. The strength you seek and the life you desire can only emerge as you leave your unhealthy, familiar surroundings and step into the world of the unknown.

SET PROPER BOUNDARIES

As you make new friends and attempt to establish healthier relationships with old ones, it is important to understand how to set boundaries. Boundaries are those imaginary lines we draw around our personal space to keep others from entering in to hurt and intimidate us. Setting appropriate limits can help you create a world of safety and self-control.

Your boundaries have been invaded by an enemy powerful enough to break through your natural lines of defense.

Your fear of possible future attacks can cause you to turn healthy boundary lines into thick walls of separation, isolation, and protection. While there appears to be safety behind these walls, the work of maintaining them in order to keep possible invaders out becomes a relentless task. Eventually these walls can become so thick they may block out your support system.

On the opposite extreme, you may feel powerless to defend yourself and eventually become incapable of protecting your personal space. You allow others to trample in and repeatedly hurt you, unsure of what boundaries to set or how to stand up for your right to maintain your personal space.

On Emory's first visit to my office, she admitted that her life was out of control. She was forty-five years old and had been in and out of relationships all her life. She was living with her fourth husband and was contemplating divorcing him.

"Every relationship I've been in has been miserable," she told me. "I feel like I have never been loved, or even respected, in any of them. My whole life, people—including my family—have used me. I never wanted to disappoint anyone. I desperately *wanted* to be loved, but I never *felt* loved. I don't feel like I even have a life. Everything I do, every decision I make, seems to be based on what *everyone else* wants or needs."

Emory was raised in an abusive home. Both her parents were addicted to illegal drugs and alcohol. Her mother and father had sexually, emotionally, and physically abused her from early childhood. If she tried to escape their abuse by saying *no* or attempting to run away, the consequences were even more severe.

Early in life, Emory's childhood experiences taught her she had no rights or power to *say no* to anyone. This early training destroyed her confidence and became the basis of her inability to set boundaries with people. In each of her marriages, Emory felt like she was nothing more than a slave. In her present marriage, her husband, Jeffery, expected her to meet all his needs without regard to her own. He dominated her, intimidating her with his demands and anger, and he insisted on making all of the important decisions in their lives. That felt normal to Emory, though, because her parents had made all the important decisions for her before she married Jeffery.

She frequently became the butt of crude remarks and jokes when she was around Jeffery's friends. On several occasions, she was informed that he bragged about their sexual life. She felt disgusted and humiliated, but he paid little attention to her pleas begging him to stop his despicable, insulting behavior.

She told me sadly, "I feel worthless. Most of the time I wish I could die."

Emory was tired of being powerless and feeling humiliated. Since she had never experienced healthy boundaries in any relationship, she didn't know what it meant to have *personal space* and to experience respect. She had always lived up to everyone else's expectations. She had been programmed by others to do whatever they wanted her to do, so thinking for herself was a foreign concept. Now she began the journey of discovering her own identity so she could experience her own desires, feelings, and choices.

Emory's new life began as she learned to gain control of her mind and as she understood she had the right to say no to others. Learning this new way to live has been a lengthy and difficult process, but with each passing day, she is making progress.

You must set and maintain healthy boundaries for yourself, your children, and anyone under your responsibility incapable of setting limits for themselves. As you do so, consider the following:

- Establish boundaries that promote personal growth and healthy relationships.

- Don't let others define the parameters of your boundaries.

- Enforce your boundaries with everyone you are in a relationship with.

- Make sure your boundaries are not so isolating that the people you have selected as supporters cannot really help you.

- Do not use your boundaries as a means to control others.

- Redefine your boundaries periodically to adjust to your changing needs.

ESCAPE DESTRUCTIVE RELATIONSHIPS

Victims often carry inside them truckloads of undeserved guilt for the problems they experience in their relationships. You may feel that you cannot leave the dangerous surroundings until you "fix" your abuser or at least resolve the issues between the two of you. So you continue to allow the perpetrator to make you feel responsible for his behavior. In this misshapen view of your role in his life, you believe you have failed somehow since you haven't accomplished the task of curing this wicked person. This distorted way of thinking will prevent you from ever being truly free.

One of your greatest fears may be abandoning your abuser in his time of need. He convinces you he can't survive without you. He claims to be on the verge of making the changes you desire, but he needs you to be there for him during the time of transition or he will never make it. He may have even threat-ened suicide to manipulate you into staying.

The abuser ignores his incessant yelling, screaming, and hitting, focusing on the times when he protected, comforted, and "loved" you. This enables him to portray your relation-ship as normal rather than something you must escape from in order to protect yourself.

You must choose to see this relationship as it is: cruel and inhuman. You need to stop listening to lies such as *He really loves me, he just has different ways of showing it*, or *He will change if I stay and help him, he just needs more time.*

If as a child you witnessed your parent being abused, you may now be staying in your harmful adult relationship sim-ply because your abused parent never left, or never took you out of the dysfunctional environment. The model you grew up with was to continue living in an abusive situation. You received the message, *No matter what happens, you stay.* Your abused parent never demonstrated effective skills for surviv-ing the adversities of life; therefore, you also lack these skills and are equally unable to enjoy healthy relationships.

You may feel disconnected from the real world. You don't believe you can survive outside your life of trauma and chaos, so you stay. But the longer you delay leaving, the more invasive the violence will become until it dominates your very existence . . . or ends your life completely.

PROTECT YOURSELF

One of the most difficult decisions you may have to make is to isolate yourself from people and situations that make you vulnerable to future attacks.

You may find that certain individuals, locations, or situa-tions cause you intense emotional suffering. You may not understand the underlying reasons for your dramatic reaction.

However, once you have identified the symptoms and their root causes, you can begin seeing connections between your past traumatic experiences and your present problematic life.

Identify the people, places, and things that send you into emotional turmoil. Isolate yourself from anyone and anything that prevents or slows the healing process.

Friends and loved ones will probably not understand what you have gone through, so they will be unable to comprehend why you have chosen to stay away from them. They cannot see the importance of distancing yourself from them in order to heal. It is possible they never will. However, remain strong and do whatever you must to remove yourself from any people or things that cause you suffering and impede your healing.

COMMIT TO THE LONG HAUL

Healing is a lifelong process. There are no quick fixes or instant solutions. You must constantly examine and confront the old ways of living. Replace faulty patterns of thinking and behaving with ones that will promote safe relationships and individual growth. True healing involves seeing yourself through new eyes—eyes that see a future filled with hope, meaning, purpose, joy, and personal fulfillment.

EXPERIENCING TRUE HEALING

*G*od has the power to heal emotional and psychological damage, no matter how severe it may be. Victims of abuse can be set free by accepting God's unconditional love and acceptance. One of the most difficult hurdles in your healing is letting go of the mistakes you have made. Because of your poor choices, you may feel guilty before the Lord, unworthy to receive His forgiveness and love. God is always willing to forgive us, regardless of what our sins are. Once you have experienced His grace, you can face your past and your future with confidence and assurance that you can be made whole.

THE FIRST AND MOST VITAL STEP

Perhaps you do not know Jesus Christ on a personal level. If that is the case, I strongly encourage you to give your heart to Him this very moment. He alone has the power to truly and completely heal you, whether your problems are rooted in physical, mental, emotional, or sexual abuse. Romans 5:1 says, "We have peace with God because of what Jesus Christ our Lord has done for us" (NLT).

Until you know Jesus Christ as Lord and Savior, you will continue to be plagued by a void in your life that can never be filled. You will live in pain, turmoil, and sin.

When God created you, He had a special purpose in mind. The first part of that plan is for you to know Him personally so you can experience peace, truth, and an abundant life, both on this earth and forever in heaven. In John 10:10, Jesus said, "My purpose is to give life in all its fullness" (NLT).

If you are not enjoying this abundant life, you need to recognize that sin is separating you from your loving heavenly Father. The abuse you suffered is not your sin. However, human nature leads all of us to choose to engage in sinful acts. God created you in His image, but He will not force you to love Him or give your life to Him. He allows all of us to choose our own pathways in life.

Whenever we go against God's will, we place ourselves in a state of distress. A sin-filled life always leads to death—eternal separation from God. Romans 6:23 (NLT) says, "For the wages of sin is death, but the free gift of God is eternal life through Christ Jesus our Lord."

You may believe that you are not really a terrible sinner, particularly in comparison to those who have sinned against you. But God's Word says, "All have sinned; all fall short of God's glorious standard" (Romans 3:23 NLT).

But because of God's compassion and unconditional love through Christ Jesus, He offers us forgiveness for our sins, abundant life, and eternal life with Him in heaven.

One of the most familiar, yet powerful verses in all of Scripture is John 3:16. It says, "For God so loved the world that he gave his only Son, so that everyone who believes in him will not perish but have eternal life" (NLT).

Today's world offers many gods, but there is only one true God. And Jesus Christ is the only way we can come to God. "For there is only one God and one Mediator who can reconcile God and people. He is the man Christ Jesus" (1 Timothy 2:5 NLT).

Jesus is God, yet He came to earth as man so that He might experience the same temptations that plague us. Still, in the midst of all these temptations, He remained without sin. "Christ also suffered when he died for our sins once for all time. He never sinned, but he died for sinners that he might bring us safely home to God. He suffered physical death, but he was raised to life in the Spirit" (1 Peter 3:18 NLT).

When Jesus died on the cross, through His battered and pain-ravished body, He paid for your sins. Salvation can be received by committing your heart and life to Jesus Christ. It is a free gift. It costs you nothing but a commitment to live your life in Christ, apart from sin.

Simply knowing about Jesus is not enough. You must choose to make him Lord of your life and believe that He died on the cross and that God raised Him from the dead. "But to all who believed him and accepted him, he gave the right to become children of God" (John 1:12 NLT).

Only when you make a true commitment to Him can a *heart change* take place. You must choose to turn your back on sin. Satan battles for your heart and mind every moment of the day. You must spend time in prayer and in God's Word each day to stand against the schemes of the enemy.

You may be thinking that you have sinned too greatly for God to forgive you. But God's grace is greater than any sin. Romans 10:9 (NLT) says, "If you confess with your mouth that Jesus is Lord and believe in your heart that God raised him from the dead, you will be saved." Four verses later, in Romans 10:13, the Bible promises that "anyone who calls on the name of the Lord will be saved" (NLT).

If you wish to accept Jesus Christ as your Lord and Savior, all you have to do is pray, asking Him to come into your heart. Admit that you are a sinner and need Christ in your life. Repent of your sins and determine not to let them control your life any longer. Then allow the Holy Spirit to lead, guide, and direct you each day.

If you're not sure what to say, you may wish to use the following prayer as a guide.

> Lord Jesus, I believe that You came to earth, died on the cross, and rose from the grave to save me from my sins so that I might have eternal life with You. Thank You for loving me in spite of all my sins, brokenness, guilt, and shame. *Thank You for understanding my pain!* I choose now to turn from the sin in my life to make room for You in my heart. Please be my Savior and Lord. Fill me with Your Holy Spirit so that I might have a passion to know You, to love You, and to live in Your will. In the name of Christ Jesus I pray. Amen!

GROWING IN CHRIST

Whether you prayed the prayer of salvation this very moment, or accepted Christ years ago but have not been living a life that glorifies Him, I encourage you to dedicate yourself to serving God and obeying the principles He has given in His Word. In order to experience true healing from your traumatic past, you must seek the holy God who created you and desires good things for you.

Many people on this earth have come to regret not walking more closely with God, but I have never met a single soul who regretted being *too* close to Him. As you draw near to the Lord, you will receive the blessings He has in store for you.

Some modern-day Christians have misinterpreted the gospel, proclaiming that walking with Christ allows believers to escape the tragedies of life. Unfortunately, those who believe this distorted doctrine tend to doubt their salvation when they experience the dark valleys of life. Since they are not in a constant state of spiritual euphoria, they may even believe the lie that they were never saved in the first place. When hard times come, they feel abandoned by God. In a state of fear and desperation, they become disillusioned and turn away from their heavenly Father at the time they need Him most.

Let me encourage you to wait upon the Lord. "Those who wait on the Lord shall renew their strength" (Isaiah 40:31 NKJV). Often, our greatest blessings come after we have gone through trials and suffering. Our pain can draw us closer to God.

During difficult times, we can choose to be obedient to God or walk away from Him. When we walk away, we lose the promises He has given us. Deuteronomy 11:25, 27 says, "No man shall be able to stand against you; the Lord your God will put the dread of you and the fear of you upon all the land where you tread, just as He has said to you . . . if you obey the commandments of the Lord your God which I command you today."

The abuse in your past can help you grow as you search for God with your whole heart. "But from there you will seek the Lord your God, and you will find Him if you seek Him with all your heart and with all your soul" (Deuteronomy 4:29 NKJV).

Whether you are a new Christian or have been a born-again believer in Jesus Christ for some time, here are a few suggestions for growing closer to Him.

Read God's Word

The Bible is God's love letter to you. Reading and studying the Word of God every day will help you get to know Christ better. This knowledge will equip you with the power and courage to overcome the effects of your abuse that hold you in bondage. Hebrews 4:12 says, "For the word of God is full of living power" (NLT). If you've never read the Bible before, the book of John in the New Testament is a good place to begin to learn about Jesus.

The power of God manifests itself in our lives through the Holy Spirit. As we stay in His Word, the Holy Spirit begins to change us into His likeness. Without the Holy Spirit, we remain powerless to change.

As you study the Bible, the Holy Spirit will begin to reveal God's plan for your life. Only in His will can you experience a life of joy and tranquility. We were created to glorify God. The greatest thing you can ever do is to share with another individual how to have a personal relationship with Jesus Christ. You can offer others the gift of eternity with a heavenly Father who will always love them and will never hurt or forsake them.

Pray without Ceasing

To "pray without ceasing" (1 Thessalonians 5:17 NKJV) means always maintaining an attitude of prayer. The deeper your prayer life, the deeper your relationship with Christ will be.

Prayer takes you into the very presence of God Himself. As His children, we have the right, the privilege, and the honor of standing before our heavenly Father or kneeling at the throne of His glory, laying our sins and our anguish at his feet. He alone can heal us, forgive us, and set us free.

The blood that Jesus shed on the cross is more than sufficient to deliver you from the devil's web of deceit and lies. Satan himself is out to destroy you and to steal your life. Prayer is your refuge from the enemy.

Pray for the Lord's leading and wisdom as you make decisions for your life. Pray that God will protect your heart from the temptations that come your way. At times when you are too tired or weak to pray, simply say the name "Jesus." There is no more powerful name in heaven or on earth.

Pray for others, and ask others to pray for you. Power is unleashed when Christians come together in prayer. "Where two or three are gathered together in My name, I am there in the midst of them" (Matthew 18:20 NKJV). Don't rob yourself of the power of prayer by allowing pride or a sense of unworthiness or shame keep you from sharing your needs with others.

Have a daily time of focused prayer, but remain in a constant state of communication and fellowship with the Lord throughout the day.

Repent of Your Sins

Jesus paid for your sin debt when He died on the cross, but simply accepting Christ as your Savior does not mean you will never be tempted again.

On our own, we are powerless to resist sin. However, that does not mean we have no choice but to continue in our wicked ways. We must call upon the Father daily, asking the Holy Spirit to provide us with the strength and discipline to stand against our sins.

When you do sin, God wants you to repent. To do this, you must acknowledge your sin and present it to the Lord, asking Him to remove it from your life.

You may not recognize some of the things that God considers sin. Here are a few examples.

• Pride

Mankind's greatest enemy is pride. Pride says, "I don't need God. I can live life on my own." Pride tells us that we don't have to give an account to God for how we choose to live. Pride will usher you straight through the gates of hell if it causes you to refuse the free gift of salvation that God has for you. Proverbs 16:18 (NLT) says, "Pride goes before destruction, and haughtiness before a fall."

Pride keeps us from taking hold of God's hand as He reaches out to us in our times of need. It can rob you of beautiful relationships with others who want to walk with you through your healing and your difficult times. Pride will keep you isolated in a world of darkness and separation. It becomes a mask, preventing others from seeing your pain.

• Sexual Immorality

The world is filled with people who walk around in pain, feeling empty and lonely inside, looking for love and meaning. Without God, what they often find is Satan's counterfeit for true love: illicit sex.

Sexual immorality is deceiving. It masquerades as power, control, and love, but it ends in guilt, shame, and failure. It robs people of their innocence and purity. And it can lead to sexually transmitted diseases, divorce, and the breakup of homes, families, churches, societies, and nations.

First Corinthians 6:18-20 (NLT) says, "Run away from sexual sin! No other sin so clearly affects the body as this one does. For sexual immorality is a sin against your own body. Or don't you know that your body is the temple of the Holy Spirit, who lives in you and was given to you by God? You do not belong to yourself, for God bought you with a high price. So you must honor God with your body."

Don't let Satan keep you trapped in your past by continuing to live in immorality. Why punish yourself by subjecting yourself to more hurt than you have already endured? Your healing will only begin when you step out of the darkness of immorality and into the light of God's love.

• Self-centeredness

Self-centeredness is commonly fueled by the anger resulting

from violence and exploitation. You feel you are entitled to receive everything you want because of all the good things the abuse in your life took away from you. But self-centeredness keeps you focused on what you feel you are entitled to rather than the real issue: your abuse.

It is natural for you to desire compensation for your pain. Self-centeredness lies to you, convincing you that the needs of others are not important, or at least not as important as your own. It can lock you in a world of revenge, greed, and isolation. Self-centeredness will keep you from investing yourself in other people's lives because their lives won't matter; only yours will.

Self-centeredness sends conflicting messages to the people who want to help you. Anger and fear become the driving forces behind your never-ending drive to retrieve the essential elements of life that were taken away from you. Sadly, this attempt comes across to others as a desire for material possessions, power, and control. In addition, your attempts to retrieve these lost parts of your life only hasten you along a self-destructive path as you make choices that cause you to repeat the cycle of abuse.

James 3:14–16 (NLT) says, "If you are bitterly jealous and there is selfish ambition in your hearts, don't brag about being wise. That is the worst kind of lie. For jealousy and selfishness are not God's kind of wisdom. Such things are earthly, unspiritual, and motivated by the Devil. For wherever there is jealousy and selfish ambition, there you will find disorder and every kind of evil."

• Distractions
One of the most powerful schemes of the enemy is to keep believers so busy they have little time to spend with the Lord. Our relationship with God is similar to other relationships we hold in high regard. We can't grow closer to people we love

unless we are willing to make them a priority by spending time with them. "Draw close to God, and God will draw close to you" (James 4:8 NLT).

• **Unforgiveness**

Unforgiveness keeps us from being set free from our pain. It becomes a stronghold that holds us captive to our past. No matter what your source of pain is, your only hope for recovery is forgiveness. It begins with looking into your past and identifying the people who have hurt you. This may be extremely painful as you face, perhaps for the first time, the fact that some or most of your pain has come from people you dearly love.

Once you identify the source of your brokenness, you must make the decision to forgive the person who abused you and then release him and your anger to God. You will then be spared the responsibility of carrying around the revenge, bitterness, rage, resentment, and grief that have haunted you.

If you are waiting for your abuser to repay you for the damage and pain he caused in your life, you are setting yourself up for a lifelong disappointment that will hold you trapped and bound to your attacker. You owe him nothing! Don't waste your priceless healing time on him.

Jesus Christ is the only One who can compensate you for the shattered dreams and injustices you have experienced. He will give you a completely new life. Once you allow Jesus to restore you, you are free to continue and complete your process of healing.

Forgiving someone who has wronged you does not imply that what the perpetrator did was right. It doesn't mean you have to have a relationship with that person. It does not mean that everything will be fine and that your pain will go away. Forgiveness is an ongoing decision that you must make from day to day.

"When you are praying, first forgive anyone you are holding a grudge against, so that your Father in heaven will forgive your sins, too" (Mark 11:25 NLT). Forgiveness is part of the healing process, but each person must come to the place of forgiveness in her own time frame. I encourage you to do so at the soonest appropriate time.

Hope in Him

The Lord does not promise that your life will be perfect and pain free. In His Word, He assures each one of us, "I know the plans I have for you . . . plans to give you hope and a future" (Jeremiah 29:11). This is the hope that can keep you pressing forward even when you see no logical way out of your troubled past.

No matter how much pain you carry, God has the remedy to heal you. He is able to do more than we can ever hope for or imagine (Ephesians 3:14–21). Psalm 146:5–6 (NIV) says, "Blessed is he whose hope is the God of Jacob, whose hope is in the Lord his God, the Maker of heaven and earth, the sea, and everything in them—the Lord, who remains faithful forever."

Through Christ Jesus, hope produces endurance and perseverance. This hope will carry you until your restoration is complete. "We continually remember before our God and Father your work produced by faith, your labor prompted by love, and your endurance inspired by hope in our Lord Jesus Christ" (1 Thessalonians 1:3 NIV).

Hope will compel you to be persistent in your endeavors to heal. Once you are healed, hope will enable you to help others who have been victimized. Hope gives you insight into your future, reassuring you that life will have meaning once again. It keeps us hanging on when the world has turned against us. Hope is the essence of life.

Fellowship with Other Believers

Surrounding yourself with other Christians will allow your faith to be strengthened as you pray and study the Word together. You will sense the power of God as you worship with other believers. Matthew 18:20 (NKJV) says, "Where two or three are gathered together in My name, I am there in the midst of them." Since God lives in the hearts and souls of Christians, we can experience His love as we fellowship with His children.

I encourage you to find a church where the gospel of Jesus Christ is preached. Attend regularly and involve yourself fully in the worship. Find local prayer groups and Bible studies that you can join.

As you get to know other believers in Christ, keep one thing in mind: They are people too. Like everyone else in the world, they're imperfect. Christians may let you down, but God never will.

If you have a bad experience in a church or other Christian group, do not give up on God. Do your best to work things out within that group. If this proves to be impossible, find a different church or group to become involved with. Don't give up on fellowship.

Trust Him Completely

Victims of abuse usually find it difficult to trust God or even sense His presence because they are emotionally disconnected from life. Detaching from the painful memories of abuse is their only escape and comfort.

We need to learn to trust God completely. Proverbs 3:5–6 says, "Trust in the Lord with all your heart and lean not on your own understanding; in all your ways acknowledge him, and he will make your paths straight" (NIV). Jesus Christ will always be your refuge and strength. "He who dwells in the shelter of the Most High will rest in the shadow of the Almighty. I will say of the Lord, 'He is my refuge and my fortress, my God, in whom I trust' " (Psalm 91:1–2 NIV).

No matter what kind of abuse you have endured, God's purpose and plan will prevail if you seek Him. Proverbs 19:21 (NIV) says, "Many are the plans in a man's heart, but it is the Lord's purpose that prevails." Trust in the Lord. He will triumph over your pain!

Seek His Guidance

Each day of your life, seek God's guidance and direction so you can glorify Him in all you do and say. When the Lord rescues someone from illness, injury, or death, He does so based on His will and purpose for that person. Once you have been healed, you owe an incredible debt of gratitude to Him. You can repay this debt by being obedient to Him and following His commandments. In John 14:15, Jesus said, "If you love me, you will obey what I command" (NIV). In the Old Testament, the prophet Isaiah said, "This is what the Lord says—your Redeemer, the Holy One of Israel: 'I am the Lord your God, who teaches you what is best for you, who directs you in the way that you should go' " (Isaiah 48:17 NIV).

True peace comes from being in God's will. Live your life to serve and praise Him.

Strive for Holiness

Holiness means moral perfection. It is an attribute that only God fully possesses. However, believers in Christ are seen by God as holy because of what Jesus Christ, God's perfect Son, did for us on the cross. Therefore, when we accept Christ, we are encouraged to live holy lives; that is, lives of clean, moral living. A life that exemplifies Christ Jesus is humble and pure, and exhibits a servant's heart.

God calls us to holiness. "I, the Lord, am your God. You must be holy because I am holy" (Leviticus 11:44 NLT). We need to strive for holiness by purging sin from our lives. While we will never attain complete holiness until we reach heaven, our goal should be to seek it with our whole heart. As we do, we draw nearer to God. We experience His power and His grace, which allow us to triumph over our pain and tragedies.

Seeking holiness opens the door for a victorious life. We will never see God in His glory and majesty without the pursuit of holiness.

I encourage you to begin your journey toward holiness today. Your heavenly Father will meet you there and guide you along the path.

Cultivate the Fruit of the Spirit

"The fruit of the Spirit is love, joy, peace, patience, kindness, goodness, faithfulness, gentleness and self-control" (Galatians 5:22-23 NIV). As these attributes become apparent in our lives, we can do great and mighty things for the kingdom of God and for those who are downcast and disheartened. Our "fruit" allows those who are hurting to see glimpses of God. It becomes their encouragement and their confidence as they struggle to regain the many things they have lost from the unbearable experiences they have endured.

Love Unconditionally

Loving people unconditionally can only be accomplished as we understand God's unconditional love for us. Before we were born, God knew everything about us. He knew our strengths as well as our weaknesses. He knew every sin we would ever commit. He knew our failures and every disgrace we would bring upon Him. Yet because of His love for us, He still accepted us, chose us to be His children, and was willing to allow His Son, Jesus, to become a sacrifice for us.

God's perfect love gives us the power to overcome the devastation in our lives. It communicates hope to the hopeless. It offers safety and security in a world filled with uncertainty and fear. "There is no fear in love. But perfect love drives out fear" (1 John 4:18 NIV). God's perfect love is our hiding place from our adversaries who are out to consume and destroy us. He tells us we are beautiful when our eyes (or other people) say we're not. He tells us we are lovable when we have never felt loved by anyone. He accepts us even when we have experienced rejection from everyone around us.

God will never leave you or forsake you. He will always be there when you seek Him. You can always count on Him. "The Lord is faithful in all he says; he is gracious in all he does" (Psalm 145:13 NLT). We are called to pass along that unconditional love to others.

Minister to Others

The best way to turn your tragedy into triumph is to allow what you've gone through to become a blessing for someone else. Sharing your experiences with others who have gone through similar traumatic incidents will help them tremendously. Just knowing that they are not alone can make a world of difference.

The more Christlike you become, the better equipped you will be to minister to those around you who are hurting. As you allow the Holy Spirit to control your life, you will become an extension of God's love to every person you come in contact with. Everyone who crosses your path carries pain. No one can escape it.

Because you have experienced a painful situation, you can empathize in a way no one else can. As you attempt to understand the pain of others, you validate their feelings. Your caring lets them know that you hear the cries of their broken heart and want to help them.

You can assure them that, even though they have gone through a dehumanizing ordeal, they have the right to be respected, valued, and loved. This will create within them the courage and determination to live free from the burdens of their past, just as you are.

Recognize God's Grace

How can we even begin to understand God's abundant grace? As long as I live I will never be able to fully comprehend all that He has done for me. Grace is unmerited, undeserved favor from God. You don't have to do anything except receive it. It is a gift; simple, yet completely incomprehensible. There is nothing we can do to earn God's grace. No amount of good deeds will bring it to you.

Perhaps you believe you are unworthy of God's grace because you walked away from Him. Maybe your abuse left you feeling dirty and bad. You may feel you can never be good enough to receive God's favor.

If you are experiencing these lies of Satan, go to God, denounce the lies of the enemy in Jesus' name, and receive God's grace. It is available to you free of charge simply by accepting it—no conditions attached.

Witness to Others

Share with others what Christ has done for you. Tell them about the hope and salvation they can have by receiving Him as their personal Lord and Savior.

There are only two qualifications for witnessing: loving Jesus and being grateful for what He has done in your life. Nothing will connect more with the heart of another person than sharing your personal experiences of how Christ has miraculously changed your life.

Don't be ashamed to share your flaws and failures with those you are witnessing to. This allows them to see and understand God's unconditional love, acceptance, and forgiveness. It opens the way for them to enter into an eternal relationship with the Lord.

As Christ calls you to witness, He also equips you to handle the opportunities He brings. His presence and power are always just a prayer away.

A CHANGED LIFE

In my private counseling practice, I see many people who have been emotionally wounded by some form of abuse. I feel blessed that God brings these people to me and that I can help them through His power working in my life. My work is often emotionally draining, but it is thrilling to see people change and heal as they allow the Father to work in their lives. In those times, everything I have been through and everything I deal with in my counseling center is all worthwhile.

I would like to share with you the story of God's healing power and grace in the life of one of my clients. His story is just one, but it represents numerous similar tales of hope and recovery.

Chuck was born into a family of violence and abuse. He has memories starting at age five of his parents getting intoxicated and attacking each other physically and verbally. He remembers sneaking out of the house at night and sleeping in the garage to get away from the violence. He has vivid recollections of lying in the car listening to loud, terrifying noises as his parents cursed and threw beer bottles and other objects at each other. Several times he tried to run away from home due to his fear of being beat to death if he did not participate with his parents as they engaged in sexual fantasies with each other.

I shook my head as Chuck shared his story with me. It was a scenario I had heard, with slight variation, countless times.

After Chuck graduated from high school he worked on a college campus in the maintenance department. His job offered him free tuition, so he spent eight years taking night classes in psychology. After graduation, he worked in a home for abused children.

At the end of Chuck's first visit with me, he told me something that made my eyes fill with tears.

"Even though I have never set foot in a church," Chuck said, "something deep inside told me there is a God, and that He loves me and has a plan and purpose for my life. Linda," he continued, "I'm here today because I am ready to let go of my past and find God's will and purpose for my life."

That day Chuck chose to face the grim facts of his past and begin the process of healing. He committed to coming in for counseling on a weekly basis. I formulated a treatment plan for him and assigned him the task of forming a support system.

This was a challenge for Chuck because he had never shared the secret of his abuse with anyone, either during his eight years of night classes in psychology or in his work at the home for abused children. He was too frightened to disclose his traumatic experiences to people he knew, so he chose to find support in a men's accountability group that focused on sexual abuse. In that group, Chuck said, for the first time in his life he felt that *someone understood his pain*. As he heard stories from other group members, he finally gained the courage to give accounts of his own experiences.

Chuck devotedly attended therapy and completed all the assignments I gave him. Over his course of healing, he regained the ability to trust. This opened the door for a relationship with Misty, a young lady he worked with at the children's facility. Two years later she became his wife.

Upon completion of counseling, Chuck decided he wanted to expand his abilities to help others recover from abuse. He attended graduate school and became licensed as a professional counselor.

Today Chuck and Misty are happily married and the proud parents of two young children. He has a busy private counseling practice and frequently speaks to groups and organizations about the devastating effects of sexual abuse.

Chuck frequently comments that he is thankful God wept with him in the midst of the tragic abuse he endured. Because of the healing the Lord provided, Chuck's life has become happier and more meaningful than he ever imagined possible.

It was my privilege to watch God transform this person, filled with hurt and pain, into a man of God who is now touching lives with the good news of the healing powers of Jesus Christ. To God be the glory. Amen!

Allow Jesus Christ to change your life. Just as He has healed Chuck and countless others, He wants to heal you. There is no tragedy, no type of abuse, no sin, absolutely nothing that could ever cause the Savior to reject you or refuse to save you. He's waiting for you to give your life to Him.

Don't let your past make you feel that He doesn't care about your pain or that you don't deserve His mercy and grace. Like a small child, run into His arms. Let Him comfort you and love you. Salvation and restoration are yours. He's already paid the price for you. Don't reject His greatest gifts: healing, freedom, and a new life in Him.

SOMEBODY UNDERSTANDS YOUR PAIN

The most important thing to remember is that *God understands your pain!* He has seen everything that has ever happened to you. He has heard your desperate cries. His heart has broken as He has watched you suffer. *He understands your pain,* because He has suffered too. He sacrificed His only Son, Jesus Christ.

Jesus left His Father in heaven to be born a human baby and live on earth so He could fully experience what it was like to be human. During his earthly life, Jesus was ridiculed, misunderstood, mocked, hated, spit on, beaten, and tortured. Those closest to Him neither understood Him nor truly believed the things He told them. In the end, He was executed in the most cruel and inhumane manner devised by man: a slow, agonizing death nailed to a cross for hours. He suffered excruciating pain—physical, emotional, and psychological—which ultimately killed him.

But Jesus Christ rose from the dead to give us life, both eternally in heaven and a more abundant life here on earth. He longs to set you free from the strongholds and bondage that have ensnared you. His heartfelt desire is for you to be truly and completely healed. He can, and will, walk with you down the pathway to a new and exciting life.

MY PRAYER FOR YOU

As we come to the end of our journey together, I am on my knees in prayer to God the Father, the Creator of everything in heaven and on earth. My prayer is that you will experience His grace in your life as never before. I pray that He will give you mighty inner strength through His Holy Spirit from the vast stores of His glorious, unlimited resources.

I pray that Christ will be at home in your heart as you trust in Him. May your roots grow deep into the soil of God's marvelous love. I ask the Lord right now to give you the power to understand how wide, how long, how high, and how deep His love really is. May you experience the love of Christ, though it is so great you will never fully understand it.

My prayer is that you will allow God to heal you, for He is indeed the only true healer.

I pray that you will be filled with the fullness of life and power that comes from God. "Now glory be to God! By his mighty power at work within us, he is able to accomplish infinitely more than we would ever dare to ask or hope. May he be given glory in the church and in Christ Jesus forever and ever through endless ages. Amen" (Ephesians 3:14–21).

FOR MORE INFORMATION

If you would like further information, please write or e-mail me:

Linda Harriss, RN, MA, M.Ed., LPC
P.O. Box 505
Brownwood TX 76804
E-mail: Lharriss@gte.net
Online: www.lindaharriss.com

I am available upon request for speaking engagements on the following topics:

My Personal Testimony
Experiencing God's Grace
What To Do with the Hurts You Don't Deserve
Seeking the Holiness of God
Establishing a Christian Marriage
Experiencing the Power of Prayer
Parenting
Abuse—Sexual, Physical, Emotional

To order Books

Additional copies of NOBODY UNDERSTANDS MY PAIN: Dealing With the Effects of Physical, Emotional, and Sexual Abuse may be ordered in the following manner:

- to order by mail: Complete this order form and mail it (along with check, money order, or credit card information) to:

  Linda Harriss, P.O. Box 505, Brownwood, TX, 76804

- to order by phone: Call (325)646-2155
- to order by fax: Fill out this order form (including credit card information) and fax to (325) 646-9361
- to order online: Go to www.lindaharriss.com

Name: _____

Address: _____

_____

Phone: _____

FAX: _____

E-mail Address: _____

Please circle one: VISA   MasterCard

Charge Card #: _____

Expiration Date: _____

Signature: _____

Books can be ordered at the following prices:

Number	Cost per book*
1-3	$15.95
4-10	$14.95
11+	$13.50

*Shipping and handling included. Allow 2-4 weeks for delivery.

Please send _____ copies @ $ _____

Sales Tax 6.25% (Texas Residents) $ _____

Total $ _____